**every
little scrap
and
wonder**

every little scrap and wonder

A SMALL-TOWN CHILDHOOD

CARLA FUNK

GREYSTONE BOOKS

Vancouver/Berkeley

Greystone Books Ltd.
greystonebooks.com

Cataloguing data available from Library and Archives Canada
ISBN 978-1-77164-466-2 (cloth)
ISBN 978-1-77164-467-9 (epub)

Editing by Paula Ayer
Proofreading by Doretta Lau
Jacket and text design by Nayeli Jimenez
Jacket photograph by Casey Horner on Unsplash
Printed and bound in Canada on ancient-forest-friendly paper by Friesens

Greystone Books gratefully acknowledges the Musqueam, Squamish,
and Tsleil-Waututh peoples on whose land our office is located.

Greystone Books thanks the Canada Council for the Arts, the British
Columbia Arts Council, the Province of British Columbia
through the Book Publishing Tax Credit, and the Government of
Canada for supporting our publishing activities.

Canadä

For my mother and brother
&
For Vanderhoof, the people and the place

A time to rend, and a time to sew...
—ECCLESIASTES 3:7A

Contents

◇◇◇

THIS IS A memoir—a work of remembering—and while I have set out to be as truthful as I can from my present vantage on the past, I know that memory is imperfect. I have purposely altered some details to preserve the anonymity of certain folks—details like names, identifying traits, occupations, and the like. I've also compressed some events and recreated dialogue for the narrative's sake. But I've tried to write with honesty, and to fit the pieces of the story to the pattern of the truth.

Patchwork Crazy Quilt

◇◇◇

EVERY SEPTEMBER, AS the last green of summer dropped to umber and rust, and the winds chilled toward frost, we ushered in the fall with a bonfire. This was no celebratory rite. This was cleanup from the season past and preparation for the winter ahead. In a clearing in the trees, on the same ground where last year's fire had burned, a pile of ashes hinted at the future. Over a starter of bark scraps, lumber odds and ends, crumpled newspapers, and a few punky blocks of wood, my dad dumped gasoline from a jerry can, then took the half-smoked cigarette from his mouth and flicked it on the heap. The spark flared to sizzle, then to high-flame shock within seconds, threatening to singe our eyelashes with the heat. When the surge had calmed enough to let my mother relax her grip on the garden hose, our purge began in earnest.

Down the trail through the trees, my brother and I dragged brushwood and deadfall. From the garden, my mother carted wheelbarrow loads of ragweed, chickweed, clover, and purple thistle. We hauled paper feed bags full of feathers and chicken heads and an assortment of creature debris that crackled like live wires when tossed into the flames. My father backed up his pickup truck as close to the burn as he could get without bubbling the paint, then stood in the box, chucking out whatever garbage had accumulated. Empty cigarette cartons, warped 8-tracks, grease rags, last autumn's Ritchie Brothers auction catalogues—the fire took it all.

After the swell of acrid smoke mellowed, we peeled willow branches, and on their whittled spear-tips jabbed half-frozen wieners, then propped them over a burning log and let the embers do their work. Weed, rot, and scrap—we fed the fire with our junk, and the fire fed us. We ate the char-dirty hot dogs roasted over a cocktail of chemicals and swore they tasted better for the blackened, ashy crust. We wore smoke in our eyes, our hair, our clothes, marking us with proof that we had eaten from the all-consuming fire and survived.

"MOST OF IT was junk," says my mother. "Most of it not worth holding on to."

Still, she holds on to the story, tells in snapshots and fragments of how she came to leave her Oregon childhood farm and move to a small town in the interior of British Columbia. At the mouth of the wide hole her father dug in the field beside the farmhouse, my mother, ten years old, stood with her seven siblings.

"You can each keep one thing," their mother had told them, "that's all we have room for."

3

Into the pit of old chairs, crockery, horseshoes, twine, shingles, worn tires, and pairs of too-small shoes, they flung in what they couldn't take—old toys, a rusted tricycle, books so warped and waterlogged the pages stuck together.

What did she take with her, I want to know, what did she save.

She tells me she can still see the wicker buggy tied with rope to the back of the overloaded truck, and the doll she held in her lap on the three-day road trip—that doll and buggy her "one thing," what she chose to save. When I ask her why they dug that hole in the first place and left so much behind, she shrugs, lifts her hands in a "who knows?" gesture. They only took what they needed. My mother can't recall the full catalogue of all they tossed into that pit—whatever's gone is gone, she says—but does remember her older brother sneaking away, not wanting his possessions to end up there. Somewhere along a creek shore where the waters run from the Gooseneck river bend, he dug his own small hole in the earth and dumped in his prized marble collection, burying the aggies and shooters, the rainbows and cat's eyes, then patted the dirt back in place and stared at it a while, as if to memorize that patch of ground for when he might return and rescue what he couldn't keep.

The doctrine of redemption runs blood-deep and won't let go. Below some suburb of swept sidewalks and tidy lawns lie artifacts of her childhood—of my mother's old life—and I want to go back, to excavate the site, dig up what's lost. I want to pick up the bits and pieces left behind and put them back together, to see the pattern in her story—our story. My story.

4   Everything that happened in life—every accident, argument, tragedy, and delight—pointed back to an ancient narrative. From the beginning, I learned to see the physical world as a shadow copy of a spiritual realm, that bigger story in which our smaller stories live and move and have their being. When I lay back on the scratchy grass to watch the sky, the clouds morphed into imagined creatures—this cumulus fluffball a fat hippo, that white wisp a lizard. From a cirrus streak to a serpent to a clue about the kingdoms of light and darkness, which were always at war, the cloud shifted, became a hint of higher meaning, like the ghost handwriting on the wall above King Belshazzar's banquet table: *numbered, numbered, weighed, divided.* Above me, all around me, the earth kept speaking, sending messages from a story that began in Eden and ended in Armageddon, authored otherworldly. When my brother and I fought over the last Fudgsicle in the freezer, and no amount of verbal wrangling could sway either of us from our respective cries of "it's mine," my mother raised a knife above it and said, "Remember Solomon?" Of course we did. No child easily forgets the two mothers arguing over the one baby left alive, both claiming that it's hers, that the dead baby belongs to the other, until Solomon calls for a sword to divide the living baby in two— one half for each mother. In our illustrated *Uncle Arthur's Bible Stories*, the wise king holds a gleaming blade above a swaddled infant, while the true mother's eyes widen in horror

and the false one's narrow to smug slits with one raised brow. In the light of my mother's allusion, the bickered-over Fudgsicle, sweating in its paper jacket, looked a little more forlorn, but neither my brother nor I surrendered. Instead, we let my mother's knife do its work and slice cleanly down the middle. We sulked away, each licking a melting chunk of chocolate ice cream on a wooden stick, tasting the splinters in what we'd been handed.

5

When my mother, at the edge of her childhood's deep hole, tossed in her box of trinkets and watched her father backfill that hole with dirt, she had no knowledge of the story that was to come. When they left behind their Oregon farm with its fields and barns and apple orchard, its forest full of climbing trees, when they auctioned off the tools and horses and milk cows to neighbours, church folks, and kin, they held the firm conviction that their family was meant to travel north. My grandpa believed it possible that the Mennonites were one of Israel's lost tribes. With this belief, every trial and persecution made sense. No wonder our people were chased out of Holland, he said, out of France, out of Switzerland, Germany, Poland, Austria, Russia. No wonder the Bolsheviks came after us with swords and guns, burned down our houses, stole back our land. No wonder our story always leaned toward exodus.

A month earlier, when Grandpa and Grandma had driven to the central interior of British Columbia on a spiritual hunch that their future lay in the Nechako Valley, sign after sign greeted them. When they arrived in the town, a stranger chopping wood in his front yard welcomed them in for lunch. He invited them to an evening service at one of the local

Mennonite churches. His wife offered them a place to sleep for the night. They knew of a farm for sale. I had a feeling about that north country, Grandpa always said. All that land. All those trees. The river flowing through the town, feeding the dirt.

6

ALREADY IN THAT small interior valley town, my dad rose early every morning and headed to work on his uncle's dairy farm. He was the eldest of nine, wore thick glasses and slicked back his brown hair like the other boys with fast cars, and though he still sat in the wooden pew on the men's side of the church every Sunday and sang the hymns in German, he snuck cigarettes and gin behind the barn, cussed behind his father's back. He was a baby when he arrived on the first train full of Mennonites, held on his mother's lap as they travelled from Swift Current, Saskatchewan—Speedy Creek, he always called it—across the flat and open prairies, through the Rocky Mountains, and into a province of trees, trees, trees. Until his own father found a house for them, they lived on the train, baked bread over a fire beside the tracks, along with the other families who'd made the journey to begin a new life in a new land, enacting all over again the Mennonite story of exodus and arrival, of picking up the pieces and putting them back together.

As if in aerial view, I see their lives converging—my dad heading west on a train across the prairies, my mother moving north, each year and mile a stitch drawing one story to the other until, at last, they meet. As my mother walks the rural road to school, my dad drives by in his Kenworth logging truck, honks the air horn, slows down, and through the rolled-down passenger window calls out and offers her a ride. In their wedding photograph, she's veiled and gauzy and shy-smiling in white. He's lean, black-suited, and turning his face away to keep the camera's flash from flaring off his coke-bottle lenses. She wonders how she got here. He wants a cigarette. She rises in the night to fix his coffee and fill his lunchbox for another night-shift long-haul logging trip down narrow black-ice roads. He brings home a stray husky and names him Butch. She lies beneath the bright overhead lights on a hospital bed and breathes until my brother slides into the world. He drives back from the bush camp to see his firstborn son. She lies beneath the bright overhead lights on a hospital bed and breathes until I slide into the world. He stands on the other side of the nursery glass and declares me the ugliest baby he's ever seen. She holds me up to the window to see the snow falling over the yard. He tosses me in the air, catches me, tosses me again. She presses her cheek against my forehead, checking for fever. He blows a scrawl of smoke into the air above our kitchen table, slams his empty milk glass down. She hums "Have Thine Own Way, Lord" while she washes the floor on her hands and knees. He cranks the volume on his pickup stereo when Johnny Cash sings "Ring of Fire."

So much seems fallen, burned, forgotten. So much tossed into the flames. But like the creed in all our scriptures, all our stories, all our songs, beauty comes from ashes, and nothing is unworthy of being redeemed. In the bread broken at the table, in the remnants of the fabric rag bag and the butchering shed's scrapings of flesh and bone, in the town dump's junk heap and the rummage sale's castoffs, memory offers its fragments. At the edge of what seems gone and lost, I want to reach back and down, take up the scraps, and buy them back with words that name them worthy.

8

To fit the broken bits into the bigger story—that's how my grandma pieced her quilts, with scraps salvaged from old clothes and fabric remnants. In the pattern of one patchwork, the family appeared materially in a rainbow of prints: an aunt's retired maternity dress, Grandpa's Sunday slacks, floral satin borrowed from a cousin's graduation gown. At her long dining room table, Grandma with her silver scissors cut out strips of cloth in every size and shape. Slivers of calico. Diamonds in stripes and plaid. Half-moons of flannel. Afternoons, no matter the season, when we stopped by for a visit on the way home from school, Grandma sat bent over the table, her thin grey hair combed back and coiled into a bun beneath the black mesh head covering pinned like a cap to her hair.

While Grandpa Funk sipped his black coffee at the head of the table and tapped his home-rolled cigarette into a beanbag ashtray, Grandma sat at the other end, puzzling over the material, lining up colours and prints, pinning the pieces together to make a larger square. She stitched the blocks, then sewed the blocks together into rows, and the rows became the quilt top. In her patchwork crazy quilt, every block looked different—purple stripes on yellow stars on flowers on plaids, reds on blacks on whites in tiny triangles, diagonal strips crisscrossing in a gridwork of fabric. On a sheet of broadcloth, Grandma laid a thin layer of wool batting and spread the quilt top over it, then sewed all the layers together, turning what began as scrap and remnant into a covering for one in need of rest.

Even now, I sleep beneath a patchwork crazy quilt stitched from the denim of my dad's grease-stained, worn-out jeans, the corduroy of my brother's school pants, my mother's closet full of skirts and slacks and blouses—all those flowers, all those greys and greens and blues—and my childhood Sunday dresses, salvaged, cut, and finally made to fit.

Even now, I lay myself down in pieces, become the handiwork, and hear that psalm sing back to me, *fearfully and wonderfully made*, as if a glowing needle pulls a thread through all the childhood years, binding all the broken parts— dead dog, lost tooth, weird hymn, burnt hand, beer breath, sad eyes, torn shirt, bloodstain, cracked bone, split lip, hard smile, junk pile, flat tire, black ice, road home, locked door— each fragment lifted from the ash and dust, set right, and given back to wonder.

AUTUMN

O Little Town

◇◇◇

I KNEW NOTHING OF my hometown's history. That the tall white wooden letters on the welcome sign at the top of the hill bore the name of the Chicago newspaperman Herbert Vanderhoof was beyond my child's mind. I had no clue that this valley town was his dream, but a failed version of it, that the artists' colony he envisioned, a haven for creatives, had come to this—a valley full of loggers, farmers, hunters, a district of 4×4's, logging trucks, dump trucks, skidders, loaders, graders, bunchers, all the heavy-duty machinery rumbling down roads en route to some bush camp work site. Ours was a town divided by the Nechako, whose name meant "big river," though I didn't know that either, nor did I know that the white sturgeon swimming the black depths of those currents were also referred to as Leviathans and Methuselahs, the oldest names we had for fish so ancient. Of those who lived here first, I hadn't heard the stories, didn't know that we called the Dakelh people "Carrier" because the widows carried the burnt bones and ashes of their men during their time of mourning. I didn't understand the narrative of colonies, fur traders, company men, traplines, treaties, shifting maps, land claims, outposts, outbreaks, heartbreak, loss.

"Of the farm"—that was the meaning of our town's name, from the Dutch and carried over from another continent, another family, another man. On our welcome sign, Vanderhoof proclaimed itself the centre of the province, the heart of it all, an X that marked the spot where some great thing might happen yet. We had no claim to fame, except the annual summer air show that swelled the town's population from 5,000 to 25,000 and cracked our skies with jet-formation contrails and stunt biplanes spiralling loop-de-loops. I sat on the roof on our fifth-wheel trailer, camping with my family in a mown, stubbled field, my binoculars trained overhead, and I felt the swell, that *wow* at how our town was shining. For that one weekend in July, the Kenney Dam was raised to let more water flow into the river, so the Nechako could show off its high current to Vanderhoof's sudden rush of visitors. Pickup trucks towing RVs and hauling campers, motorhomes and station wagons, carloads full of kids and dogs and red-faced parents— they poured into the open acres of shorn hayfields rented out by local farmers to hold the air show horde, my family among them. We joined the throng for the three-day event, living in our trailer, flanked by relatives and friends and thousands upon thousands of strangers who turned our town into a city staring up at the sky, witnesses to spectacle.

Leaning back in his lawn chair in the trailer's shade, my dad would tap his cigarette ash into his empty brown bottle and say, "You just wait. You just wait for them Snowbirds to fly."

The Snowbirds were the air show's closing act, the grand finale, and my dad's version of a celestial sign and wonder: that squadron of aerobatic jets sent by the Canadian Armed Forces to demonstrate military precision in the glory of the skies. When they started their engines for takeoff, my dad stood at the barbed-wire fence along the runway's edge, one man among the rows and rows of onlookers. As the Snowbirds roared and rose, wings catching the sun, my dad adjusted his ballcap and shielded his eyes, following their V formation until they banked, grew smaller in the blue, then disappeared, leaving us with "Spirit in the Sky" blaring from speakers mounted high on the hydro poles. I made my way to him—my dad transfixed, standing there in his white undershirt and dark-blue work pants, and when the rumble started up again, far off and faint, I squeezed in front of him, leaned into a smooth, unbarbed section of the wire fence, and together we waited, waited, waited until—there, there! I pointed to the black specks overhead, and down they rumbled with such noise I clapped my hands to my ears. My dad whooped and punched a fist into the air like a revival-tent amen. We cheered, clapped, hollered for the Snowbirds, sleek and loud and perfectly aligned in their fly-by majesty. From their view and vantage, we must have looked like weeds in a field, rooted to the earth, and me with my white-blonde hair like a dandelion blossom gone to fluff, here today and gone tomorrow, the way the crowds appeared at the air show's opening and vanished as the Snowbirds flew away.

Through the speakers, the announcer crackled his enthusiastic thanks and farewell and see you next year, and the national anthem played us out, a swelling soundtrack for the great exodus from the litter-strewn fields: dust clouds and exhaust fumes and a bumper-to-bumper migration inching along the road into town, creeping over the bridge, through the traffic light at Stewart and Burrard, across the train tracks, and back up the hill toward home.

Whatever grandness and glitz our town gained during the air show weekend receded like the river, quick as a dream. The streets went quiet again. Pickups idled in the Co-op parking lot. The dust and dry weeds of late summer shifted to frost-glitter on the fields in the morning and a fat, low-hanging harvest moon at night. Along the highway ditch, the scrawny man in the cowboy hat and boots buttoned his flannel jacket to the throat against the coolness as he walked with his garbage bag slung over his shoulder, bending every few feet to pick up another empty, making his way toward the depot at the back side of the laundromat, where a man named Diamond Jim exchanged cans and bottles for cash.

WHEN I SPUN our plastic light-up globe, I couldn't even find Vanderhoof. On most maps, it was a pinpoint, its name so small I needed a magnifying glass to find it, but still, I loved it. All of it. Its streets and buildings, the lettering of signs in storefront windows, the busted-up winter-thrashed sidewalks whose cracks I tried not to step on for fear of breaking my mother's back. Every store and shop held for me a clear and peculiar feeling. In the same way that a song like "This Ol' Riverboat," with its jangly tambourines and sunny harmonies, conjured in me a golden warmth, or the tinny trumpet of "Red Roses for a Blue Lady" left me hollow and tight-throated, every building I passed or entered gave off its own mood and tone. Taylor Brothers Hardware felt like Saturday-morning chores, mostly boring, but full of brightness—all those shiny washers, bolts, nails, and screws. Royal Foods was lit with possibility; if Tante Nite was working, she might slip me a free chocolate or cluster of grapes. The bank stretched out like Sunday sermons, blank and full of the same long waiting only to listen to words that held no meaning for me—*overdraft, transfer, withdrawal, interest.* But Toyland owned all the confetti-cake joy of a birthday party. At the corner of the two main streets, in a narrow storefront that once housed a perpetual church rummage sale and would eventually become Black Bob's Billiards, a seedy arcade where all the troublemakers hung out, Toyland beckoned every child with its rainbowed bubble-lettered sign. Inside—dolls, trucks, Tinker Toys, boxes of the latest Lego, racks of die-cast metal cars, cap guns, squirt guns, rolls of stickers, bags of marbles, bins of rubber balls in neon colours, parachute men, army figures, whistles, balloons—a wish list come to life.

"You have ten minutes," our mother would say, and then showed me and my older brother her wristwatch so we knew our starting time. As we walked the aisles and eyed the shelves, holding up items for each other to see—"Check out this air rifle!" and "Whoa—remote control!" and "I'm gonna save up pop bottle money to buy this!"—I felt both the adrenaline of high hope and, as our minutes wound down, the inner sigh of resignation. Three dollars in a plastic change purse emblazoned with "Jesus Loves Me" only bought so many marbles or stickers and was never enough for the electronic Speak & Spell computer with a robot's voice that said *You are correct!* whenever I punched in the right answer.

18

Farther down the block, the Department Store's double glass doors opened to a realm that left me with the breezy pleasure of a new haircut's flounce and curl. In the store, I felt dressed up, grown up. The word "department" seemed to me a formal word, a city word, one that might appear in a movie about New York or in a book about a rich girl who lived in a high-rise apartment. The Department Store was the only store in town with wall-to-wall carpeting, which added an air of luxury, especially when I tromped over the orange-and-yellow diamond pattern in snowy winter boots.

Racks of clothing, shelves of footwear, and display cases of costume jewelry took up most of the store's space, but in the back corner was the section I loved best—fabric and notions. Here, I ran my fingers over lace, ribbon, rickrack, and buttons, turned the glossy pages of pattern books, and followed my mother down rows lined with bolts of calico and flannel, silk and brocade. At the cutting counter, a woman with silver shears and a measuring tape draped around her neck rolled out fabric and cut it into the length required for whatever my mother was sewing. The sound of the scissors slicing cleanly through the cloth was the beginning of something new—a Christmas dress for me, a blouse for my mother.

One block over and down lay the post office, cool and aloof and satisfyingly eerie. Before we entered, we paused a moment to look at the pieces of paper taped to the glass front doors. Here, photographs of the newly deceased were displayed, along with their death dates and upcoming funeral details. My mother read to me the names, told me if and how we were related, and then said what she always said if there were only one or two announcements: "Deaths always come in threes. You just wait. Someone else will die soon."

The post office made me feel like I was inside a story in the pages right before a mystery was about to be solved. I loved it when my mother let me go in there alone with her ring of keys. On the concrete floor, my footsteps echoed, and the walls of small numbered mailboxes felt like clues. When I slotted the key into our box, turned it, and opened the little door, I could see beyond the envelopes into the inner world of the mailroom, where torsos of women at work bustled by and boxes, parcels, and stacks of more envelopes waited to be sorted. Once, as I looked through the portal of the open mailbox, a face appeared. With only one eye and part of a nose in view, it looked like a cutaway from my nightmares, a demon winking through. When the eye met mine, a lady's voice screeched in surprise. I slammed the metal door and, with shaking hands, slipped in the key, locked it, and ran back to the car.

So much of the town remained hidden, and it left me feeling small and curious about what I didn't know. The law office, the courthouse, Frankie's Pub—places like these existed in the empire of the unknown. I watched for people going in and out of doors to these mystery buildings, searching for a familiar face. What was Bud's Electric, and who was Bud? What did people eat at The Chuckwagon Café? Who slept in the beds of the Reid Hotel? But I never asked these questions aloud, only let my imagination work them over into a personal mythology. Bud's Electric became a shop owned by a bald man with flowers that plugged in and lit up, and chandeliers whose glass pendants dangled in the shapes of tulips and roses. Frankie's Pub, I imagined, belonged to a man with a mustache and a huge room full of bumper buggies, the word "pub" sounding to me like the rubber punch of carnival cars bouncing off each other. If we happened to drive past on a late weekend evening and I saw out my backseat window a cluster of women and men huddled and smoking in the cold air, I looked for one who might be Frankie, a mustached man with the keys to all the cars.

The town, sprawled over a grid of streets that stretched beyond my experience, seemed to me inexhaustible. There were still alleys and streets I'd never walked down, whole neighbourhoods bordering the core that were full of houses full of families full of kids whose names I didn't even know. On the outskirts and beyond were the rural districts—Sinkut, Mapes, Cluculz, Braeside, all geographies that marked the people who lived there. To live out at Mapes meant you raised livestock, usually hogs, sheep, and cattle, and definitely horses. To be from Cluculz Lake made you backwoods tough and tuned to wildness. Those around the base of Sinkut Mountain hunted, held traplines, and fished the creek. The Braeside families farmed in wide-open, river-fed fields of wheat, hay, canola, and barley, and raised dairy herds. We drove the narrow gravel roads, passed acres and acres without a single house in sight, until the world looked uniformly uninhabited. But the town itself—the village centre—full of people whose daily work dressed them up in ironed shirts and slacks, blouses and skirts—teachers, municipal workers, bank clerks, and insurance brokers—remained the true exotic.

That the world could be this close and yet so full of secrets magnified its allure. Like when the preacher spoke words like transfiguration, sanctification, justification—all those "-ations"—and read from the Bible those names so strange they seemed like a spell—Mephibosheth, Zerubbabel, Abednego—like other realms still veiled and obscured to me, the town held back its hidden stories. When we passed the old hospital on our way from Sunday-evening church, my mother, at the wheel, pointed at the building and said, "That's where they kept the bodies." My brother and I leaned forward in our seat, waiting for more. "Some people say it's haunted," she said, and then told us again about the year she worked as a nurse's aide at the old St. Joseph's Hospital. In the basement, at the far end of the building, was the morgue, where all the dead were stored in long metal drawers. Sometimes, she said, the nuns came to wash and prepare a body for burial, and to say a final prayer. In their long black robes, they seemed to float down the dim hallway, rosaries swinging as they walked. In the night-shift hours, no one wanted to go to the basement. The nurses swore they'd seen and heard strange things. An empty wheelchair rolling down the hall. The sound of footsteps. Creaking doors slamming shut when no one was around. A child crying for her mother.

Down the hill and across the bridge we drove, past the St. Joseph's parish, with its low-roofed school, church, and convent housing. On the radio, quiet through our car speakers, a man's voice intoned on a singing single note, *Hail Mary, full of grace, the Lord is with thee.* His voice turned everything misty, as if we had drifted inside a cloud of incense. The autumn fog rising from the river knit us together into mystery. My mother shook her head at the radio's strangeness, reached out with a quick hand, and clicked the dial off. Behind us, the Catholic church vanished in our wake. Down the main street with its blackened store windows and empty sidewalks, through the green of the town's single traffic light, we rolled. The night train's long, slow whistle sounded, a far-off moan wearying toward us through the dark. If I leaned my head back against the seat and closed my eyes, I could see them still, those nuns floating in their black-and-white robes, their swinging rosaries, and I could hear the steps of someone walking, the doors swinging open to even more rooms, and the sound of a girl calling out from a hidden place on the north side of the river.

Where I
Come From

◇◇◇

THE WHOLE HOUSE sang with the voices of women—chatter in motion as they scurried from kitchen to dining room to living room and back to kitchen with napkins, dishes, glasses of fizzy punch, and laughter, at ease as they perched on stack stools, one pantyhosed leg crossed over the other. Aunts, great-aunts, grandmas, a great-grandma, cousins—first and second and third—abounded, as did the Bible-study and sewing-circle ladies from the church. A shriek and holler sounded by the stove, and there stood Aunt Mary with her white half-slip bunched around her ankles. Behind her, Auntie Margaret laughed and pointed. This was the standard family kitchen prank: sneak up, reach beneath a woman's skirt, and pull down her undergarment. When the uncles tried it, spatulas slapped the air and wooden spoons flew, but when the women did it to each other, we all thought it was hilarious.

I'd come for the finger foods, the glass platters of marsh-mallow balls, fudge squares, antipasto on fancy crackers, dishes of olives and trays of meat, pinwheel sandwiches with Cheez Whiz and a slice of dill pickle rolled into the centre, and the huge watermelon my mother had decoratively knifed into a jagged basket filled with chunks of fruit.

I circled the table, the youngest of the guests except for the new baby, a pink swaddled lump that drew the women to hover over it with their *oohs* and *oh buts*. In the corner of the living room, amid a swag of pink crepe paper streamers and pink balloons, flanked by stacks of presents wrapped in various shades of pink, in a rocking chair plumped with pillows, sat my distant cousin Darlene, nursing her week-old daughter.

Because of the flannel receiving blanket draped over Darlene's torso, I couldn't see the baby, nor the breast. Always, the female body remained hidden. Beyond my own body and the occasional flesh-coloured blur of my mother as she darted from the bathroom to her bedroom, half-clad in a too-small towel, the most I'd spied of the female form was in the under-wear section of the Sears catalogue, where women in pale girdles and brassieres smiled at something unseen, off camera, with their long-lashed mystery eyes.

It would be years before I'd hear the anatomically correct names for private body parts. For now, my mother referred to everything as a "peeter," as in "what you pee with." Everyone had a peeter, and you kept your peeter covered and quiet.

You didn't talk about your peeter, unless you had trouble with it. Then you went to your mother and said, "My peeter hurts," and she handed you a tin of diaper-rash cream and said, "Here. Try this."

With all the men named Peter whom I knew, the word and what it denoted became confusing. Great-Uncle Pete, my dad's brother Peter, Peter Wiens, Peter Giesbrecht, Peter, Paul and Mary. I supposed they had peeters, too, but I couldn't imagine them, even though I tried. When someone called out, "Peter!" at a family gathering, across any room, I held back my laugh, but barely, and tried not to look my brother in the eye for fear we'd both burst and be scolded, grounded, no *Wonderful World of Disney* tonight.

"Do you want to hold the baby?" said a voice behind me. Aunt Sharon, the new grandmother, shuffled me and my over-flowing plate toward the rocking chair. "Sit down," she said, and patted the sofa, took my food from me, and lifted the pink lump from Darlene.

I took the baby as I would an armload of firewood, like a log in a forklift's grip, cradled.

"Be sure to hold her head," said Darlene, her hands out-stretched as if to steady me.

But I knew this baby rule, that they had soft and lolling heads, and if you didn't hold them right, you'd snap their necks or make them brain damaged. This baby, the one mouthing the air with milk-lips, arched her back, clenched her fists near her cheeks, and stuttered out a cry.

"Are you pinching the baby?" said Aunt Sharon. She gave me a stern eye, hands on hips, then laughed.

"She's just gassy," said Darlene. The baby's rear end rumbled against my forearm.

"You can have her back," I said, and inched forward on the sofa cushion, but Darlene said, it's okay, you can hold her for as long as you want. Just rub her back, said an aunt, pat her bum, hum to her, but hold her head, they said, her neck is weak, and put this blanket on your shoulder just in case she barfs.

THE NEXT DAY, on the bus ride home from school, I slid in beside my assigned seatmate, Tasha Penner. She was a year older, attended the public school up the road, and wasn't forced to wear a navy-blue polyester jumper every day. But she, too, was Mennonite, so we knew we were probably related, somehow, way back on our fathers' sides. Tasha was loud, large-limbed, the kind of girl my mother called "a handful," and she was completely unafraid of the older boys who hissed names at us from the back of the bus and shot their spitballs through drinking straws when Mr. Jordan, the driver, wasn't watching.

"I got to hold a baby last night," I said. "Newborn."

Tasha hunched down in the seat and leaned in close. "You know how babies are born, right?" she said.

I nodded. I knew. "From bellies?"

I'd seen the swollen stomachs of my aunts and the ladies at church, standing with a hand pressed to the growing roundness or against the small of the back, their pregnant shapes belling out inside their vast dresses as they shuffled. And when the baby showed up, their bellies, like risen bread dough punched down, sagged back into place, hidden beneath generous folds of fabric.

"Nope," Tasha said. "Not from bellies. My sister Candace just had a baby, and she had to push it out." Here, Tasha thrust her face right close to mine, her breath hot and smelling like tuna sandwich. She whispered, the words coming out in rhythmic pulses: "She *had* to *push* it *out* her *bum*."

Revelation in childhood comes in strange and unexpected ways, like a pair of metal scissors jammed blades-first in an electrical outlet—a shock, a spray of sparks, and a bright shudder that, for hours after, leaves the body abuzz.

"Her *bum*?" My voice came out thin, choked.

"You have to push a baby out of your butthole. You have to push *really* hard," said Tasha. "Like when you have to go *really* big. You have to push even harder than that. *Way* harder." She leaned back and nodded.

I tried to picture it. A woman on a toilet, and a baby easing out into the dirty flush and swirl. Then I tried to not picture it. Impossible, I thought. I'd held the newborn, Nicole. Her floppy pink head was bigger than an orange, bigger than a grapefruit, too big to fit.

"It's true," said Tasha. "That's what my sister Candace had to do. She had to push Bradley out her bum."

On that ride home, with the late-September sun cooking the bus to stuffiness and sticky vinyl seats, dressed in holy uniform like all the other Christian-school girls, suddenly carsick and sweltering in my polyester jumper, white knee socks, and Buster Brown shoes, I vowed I'd never have a baby, never let one grow inside my belly, and never push one out that hole.

"HOW WAS SCHOOL?" my mother asked. I set my orange Muppets lunch kit on the counter, opened it, took out the balled-up waxed paper, and chucked it in the trash.

28 "Fine," I said. "How was I born?"

"How were you born?" My mother paused at the kitchen sink, her hands still dunked in the suds. "What do you mean, 'how were you born'?"

"How did it happen?" I wanted to hear her side of the story, her version of events.

"Well," she said. "I guess I went to the hospital. Your aunt Carol dropped me off. And then—well, then you were born."

I waited for more details, but she gave up nothing.

"That's it?" I said. "I was just born?"

"Then Dad drove back from bush camp and came to the hospital."

This part of the story I knew well. My dad told it often, especially in the presence of dinner guests and at family gatherings.

"I looked through the window where all the babies were sleeping," he'd say, "and I said to the nurse, 'That one can't be mine! She's the ugliest one in the nursery!'" And then he'd laugh and laugh, and an uncle would say, "Is that right, Zusa?"—a play on my middle name, Sue, and the Low German word for sugar.

In the living room, I sat on the rug in front of the bookcase, pulled out the photo album with the red and black velvety flowers—my album—and opened to the first page of pictures. Me, pink-faced, fat, hairless, swaddled in a white blanket and lying on a pillow next to a vase of red carnations.

My mother stood over me. "Your father sent those flowers."

In the next photograph, he sat on a dining room chair and held me on his lap, a box of Corn Flakes foregrounded on the table beside him, as if we were a Kellogg's breakfast ad. More photographs of me blue-eyed and bald, smiling into space, chewing on a pink stuffed cat, grabbing at my brother's face. But no further clues as to the birth. No pictures of my mother clutching her swollen stomach. None of her grimacing on a hospital bed. No toilet. Nothing to confirm or deny Tasha's story.

My mother sat down on the couch and turned on the TV for the last half of *The Young and the Restless*. "What are you looking for?" she said.

In cartoons, a flapping stork dropped its bundle on a doorstep, through a bedroom window, or right into a crib—a fairy-tale joke, I understood, but why the secrecy, and why the lowered voices at the edge of the kitchen where all the pregnant aunts clustered together whenever the family gathered? They rubbed their bellies, fat with the knowledge of how we all arrived.

Where I came from began with that first damp patch of Genesis earth, God scooping and sculpting that dirt to make a creature, then blowing his breath into it to turn it human. But that origin was bound to another story that had bloomed in my mind, one of babies floating around in Heaven like balloons without strings, waiting to be born. All it took was a husband and a wife to say, "We're having a baby," and somehow—and this had been the mystery until now—somehow, God plucked a floating baby from the air and fired it down

29

through the clouds, the way we chucked stuffed animals down Grandma's laundry chute. Out the baby came, into the arms of its mother, but first, the pushing. Oh, the pushing.

"Did you have to—" the words stuck. "Push me out?"

My mother cough-sniffed, muted the TV, and looked over at me and the open album. "Push you out?" A series of other noises sputtered forth—*pffft*, *chk*, *uhf*—and finally, "Well, yes, I—I guess I did—push you out. And then you were born. Do you want some cookies and a glass of milk?"

NO PHOTO SHOWED her pregnant. In one, she stood in a white dress at the front of Gospel Chapel, clutching a bouquet of roses, her long brown hair beneath a gauzy veil, my dad beside her in his skinny black suit and thick black-rimmed glasses, his thinning hair slicked back, ducktailed. When I flipped the page, she stood next to him again, this time in a purple flowered dress, my brother balanced between them on the shiny chrome bumper of my dad's new logging truck. But mostly, my mother stood outside the frame. When I asked where were the ones of her round belly, the ones with me inside, she'd say that the Amish don't like to have their picture taken, as if she still held her ancestors' view that posing for a photograph meant pride swelled in the soul.

"Besides," she said, "I was the one taking all the pictures."

I wondered if this was her cover for never having carried me at all, if she wasn't telling me the true story. That I came from somewhere else. Someone else. Even though Mrs. Bergen had never been pregnant, she and Mr. Bergen showed up at church one Sunday with a baby in their arms—a girl they named Elizabeth, born from a different mother who lived in Manitoba and who didn't want to keep her, and so they adopted her. On the sanctuary bulletin board beside the staircase to the nursery, Elizabeth's photograph, along with her name and birthday written in fancy black script on a pink card, were thumbtacked to the cradle roll, which announced all the fellowship's new babies.

My name, too, had been listed on a pink card, and my arrival announced like good news. My mother had carried me into the sanctuary, been swarmed by the women who wanted to get a look, to peel back the folds of the blanket and see my fat pink cheeks. Before me, it had been my mother, swaddled in her own mother's arms. And before her, my grandmother, pink and small and bundled. Back and back we went, my mother, her mother, and the grandmothers long dead, tethered by the same cord strung beneath a sky that stretched from river valley to canyon to coast to plains, replicating and aglow across a continent and ocean, back into the dust and stars, back into the holding pen of Heaven, where another one waited to swing down on the line, come sliding into the doorway of the world, her body, my body, and whoever came next.

"See?" my mother said. "Here's one of me holding you." She pointed to a picture of me on her lap in the rocking chair, my brother squished in beside her on the seat, fighting for space. My cheeks flushed, my eyes wide and shining red, stunned by the camera flash. And looking down at me with an almost smile, my mother, green-eyed, younger, her shoulder-length brown hair pulled back from her face.

While I studied the picture, she headed back to the sink full of dishes and the pots simmering on the stove. The hunch gnawed deep, a question mark, a pang.

32 "Come, have something to eat," my mother called from the kitchen.

There was more to the story, more that I wasn't being told. I turned the pages and saw myself in miniature—pale and fuzz-headed, lying in a crib with that pink stuffed cat in my grip, chewing on a squeaky toy, cruising in the walker, sucking on a bottle, crawling on the linoleum in pursuit of my brother. In photo after photo, I repeated like an echo, starting small but growing, the way the belly grew and swelled. I'd come from far away, all the parts of me composed from other parts, like hand-me-downs turned into scraps and ready for the sewing. My eyes the same blue as my grandma's mother, my hair the colour of my Tante Nite's, my turquoise veins bright as my dad's on the sallow skin beneath his shirtsleeves. If I really looked, I saw it—where I'd come from, who carried me here. At the table waited my place, the food laid out for me, my glass already poured full.

My Father's
World

◇◇◇

N THE SATURDAY morning hours, before the yard filled up with the smokestack exhaust and engine rumble of Peterbilts and Kenworths, before all the loggers returned from their shifts and before my dad was home to shoo me back toward the house, I headed across the yard pocked with fallen leaves and pine cones, dodging the small puddles potholed in the gravel driveway, and snuck into the side door of the shop. I stepped over the threshold and into darkness. Friday night's woodstove fire had gone to ashes, and the concrete floor beneath me had cooled in the night. The building's only light shone from a strip of windows in the bay doors. Gone were the usual hiss of the air compressor, the tire gun's jolt, and the flying sparks from the welder's torch. Tools, chains, hoses, and cords dangled from hooks. Machines whose names I didn't know lay propped against the walls. The only sound was the hum of the refrigerator and the scuff of my footsteps echoing.

At the far end of the shop, a staircase led to a small balcony. When I climbed the steps, I felt the same thrill as when I wandered alone inside the empty church on cleaning days. While my mother vacuumed and dusted the basement of the church, I would tiptoe through the sanctuary, snooping behind the pulpit, turning the pages of the preacher's huge black Bible, reaching my hand into the velvet offering bags passed around each Sunday by the ushers, feeling for lost coins. In my dad's shop, on the balcony overlooking the work bays, I opened and closed the tiny plastic drawers that lined the shelves. Nuts, bolts, screws, washers—the cold silver in my hands felt like money. I sorted them into small piles and clinked them together in my palm, dreaming myself rich, but on edge, listening for a logging truck heading up the driveway and my dad returning home.

We called it *the shop*, though no goods or services were for sale there. If anything was bought or sold at the shop, it was done by swap or dicker, as in "I'll give you fifty bucks for that wheel rim" or "How about a case of beer for a hunk of moose?" When we moved to the five acres off Kenney Dam Road, the first thing my dad built was his shop. He was tired of renting space in someone else's truck garage and wanted to buy a second logging truck—to be not just a log-hauler, but a company owner with a crew that drove for him.

The shop was big enough to hold two logging trucks with their empty trailers loaded on the backs. The double-bay doors raised and lowered on a pulley system, the metal chains jangling a silver echo off the concrete floor every time some-one yanked them up to open. By my dad's command, the chains were off-limits to me.

"You're not strong enough," he said. In a child's grip, the chains could easily slip and the door come slamming down.

"It could crush you," said my dad.

The threat alone became a magnet that drew me to the chains. When my dad wasn't watching, I slipped them out from behind their holding hook on the wall and pulled just enough to let in a crack of light. As I lowered the door, I held the chains taut, careful to anchor myself to make sure it didn't thud when it shut. I could feel the weight of it. *It could crush you.* I pictured myself splayed across the threshold, the door slicing down, cleaving my torso in two, guts spilled on concrete.

This was my father's world—big rigs, horsepower, air horns, oil drums, tire guns, ratchets, rad hoses, woodsmoke, whisky, country crooners, raunchy laughter, and ashtrays brimming with ash and smouldering cigarettes. The shop was a world of men in coveralls, in grease-stained work pants and snap-front shirts, in steel-toed boots, and in ballcaps crested with logos for Aro Automotive and Pine Country Inn. My dad had his own line of ballcaps printed, royal blue with a white crest, and in bright block letters: *Dave Funk Trucking, Ltd.* He handed out his hats like handshakes or high-fives, eager to impress, to draw a new fan to his social crew. In his world, goodwill toward men was a freely given ballcap bearing his name. When he passed a man in town sporting one of his company hats, he nodded and lifted two fingers from the steering wheel in a kind of peace-salute hello and gesture of approval.

Old Alec with one glass eyeball. Doukhobor Joe. The Jakes, all three of them with dark-tinted glasses and puffy sideburns. They were members of the crowd that congregated at the shop, coming and going with their loud trucks. They borrowed my dad's tools to do what monkey-wrenching needed to be done before the next shift in the bush, and after the work was finished, they hung around to pass a bottle of whisky or share a case of beer. Falcon, the pock-marked, lanky trucker, whose fear of snakes led my brother and me to chase him around the shop with a plastic cobra until he scrambled into his cab and refused to come out, even after we put the toy away. Clem, slit-eyed and always smiling, rosy-cheeked, with a kind, red-lipsticked wife who wouldn't leave her house. Pack-sack Lewis, who lived in a travel trailer on the far side of the driveway and taught my brother how to trap squirrels, then skin them and stretch their tiny hides on homemade tanning frames built from twine and sticks. Sparky, who didn't drive truck but knew all the loggers, who came for the free booze and always offered to finish off whatever bottles my dad had stashed away.

The shop crew loved their rye and Cokes, their rum and Pepsis, their Pilsner and Molson and O'Keefe Extra Old Stock. The squat white fridge in the corner by the woodstove displayed rows of labels peeled from Royal Reserve whisky bottles and stuck on the door. I counted the black squares with the red maple leaf and A PROUD CANADIAN lettering over and over, never getting the same number twice.

Between the woodstove and the fridge, half a dozen blocks
of wood formed a ring, with the biggest block at the centre.
These were the makeshift barstools and card table where the
men played "Stop the Bus." Three quarters to play, three cards
to a hand. Collect the same suit, and the first player whose
cards add up to thirty-one stops the bus. Loser pays a quarter. I didn't understand all the rules, what it meant to "knock"
and "pay the driver," but I loved to watch the empty ashtray
fill with quarters, to see a cussing man kicked off the bus
and out of the game while the other men laughed at him and
raised their bottles in a mock toast.

I watched my dad's mood for signs that he might let me in.
If I offered to clean the shop bathroom and scrub the sink of its
black grease and the toilet of its spatter and scum, if I leaned
on his shoulder, if I sweetened in his presence, then he might
let me hold his hand of cards and throw down a jack of spades,
draw an ace, then knock on the wood to signal the final round.

"Rugrat," he said. "You little potlicker, come here."

I didn't care what name he called me, only that his voice
was soft when he said it, not the voice that hardened to *get
outta here* and a hand waved toward the door. Not *you're in
the way* or *go home and help your mother*.

He let me perch on his knee so that he could see the cards
I held and tell me when to draw and what to throw away.
When I said I was thirsty, he passed me his bottle for a sip. The
other men talked above me, puffed their cigarettes, laughed,
slammed down their hearts and diamonds, paid their quarters to the pot. When the final round ended, and all the men
had lost their money, and I was the only one left on the bus,

my dad picked up the ashtray and dumped the coins into my hand.

"Better take that home before you lose it," he said, and nodded toward the house.

The bay doors hung half-cocked on their chains, and in the dusk, light from the shop rolled the warped shadows of trucks and trailers into the yard. I walked from the shop to the house with the quarters jingling in my coat pocket and the bitter, yeasty taste of beer still on my tongue. My breath in the night air whitened like a puff from a cigarette, like smoke from my father's mouth. Up ahead, past the garden's black soil tilled over after harvest, against a backdrop of wind-stripped birch and poplar, framed in the light of the kitchen window, my small, aproned mother stood, stirring and slicing, cooking to a Hagood Hardy piano solo wavering on an 8-track. *How long until your father comes home*, she would ask me. I never knew the answer. *Pretty soon*, he always said, *pretty soon*.

Between the shop and the house, I followed the groove he'd worn in the gravel, morning and midday and evening, as ritual as prayer before meals and sleep. As a boy, he must have followed a path his own father walked before him, to the barns, the woodshed, and the fields, carrying back to the house the buckets full of milk or an armload of kindling. When I reached into my pocket, the coins slid coolly through my fingers, proof of where I'd been, where I'd come from. Behind me, voices crackled and hooted, the talk and laughter of men hunkered on old stumps around a woodstove's fire, their sound drifting out into the falling night. Among them, my dad, calling for one more game of cards, one more round of drinks.

First God

◇◇◇

CAN STILL SEE them in their circle of hardback wooden chairs, heads bowed over the onionskin pages of the King James, those women of the Wednesday-morning Bible study. In church-soft voices, they read aloud from Psalms and Proverbs, the prophets and epistles, following a paper script with questions for discussion. While they prayed and softly spoke, I roamed the building freely. Downstairs, I marveled at the men's urinals, flushed every toilet. Sprayed the can of aerosol deodorizer until the room smelled like a chemical bouquet. In the upstairs nursery, I crawled into a crib, trying to remember what it felt like to be a baby. I tugged the plastic cow by its string and made it moo. I stacked a tower of wooden blocks and made it topple. In the Sunday-school rooms, I snooped through stacks of coloured construction paper, sniffed the pots of white glue, stood at the front of the class and pretended I was the teacher, telling a flannelgraph story with boils, locusts, and blood.

Upstairs in the sanctuary, the women told their own stories, pored over the scriptures, sniffled into Kleenexes and touched one another's hands, and prayed on. Afterward, there'd be fellowship in the basement kitchen, tea and weak coffee, friendship cake and matrimony squares and egg-salad sandwiches cut cleanly into triangles, but first, they studied, bent over their Bibles with the devotion of ancient scholars, these Anns and Tinas, Sarahs and Netties, grandmas and never-marrieds and stay-at-homes with school-aged kids. Among them, my mother, quiet, smoothed her skirt and bowed her head.

She was one of the church's devout, a Wednesday-morning Bible study lady and a Tuesday-evening sewing circle member, a volunteer in the church nursery and a Sunday-school student in the adult class. Every morning at the breakfast table, she read to us from *Devotions for the Family*, a slim paperback she bought at Streams of Life, the Christian bookstore and gift shop run by the preacher's wife. Monday through Friday, as my brother and I gummed our oatmeal and chewed our toast, we heard about Jack and Jeanie, twins who sinned, confessed, repented, and were forgiven, all within a two-minute story. At the end of it, she read the daily Bible verse, which we repeated back to her until we could say it without mistakes. Sometimes, before the breakfast devotional, I'd stand at my mother's bedroom door, peeking through the crack to see her kneeling by her bed, forehead propped on her clasped hands, slim black Bible lying open beside her. Then she'd rise, run through her exercises—toe touches and bicycle legs pedalling in the air as she lay on her back, counting aloud through her panting and puffing.

She was, I believed, exactly the woman King Solomon described in the book of Proverbs, the one worth far more than rubies. Like that Proverbs 31 woman with her litany of virtues, my mother provided food, worked with her hands, tilled the field, kept her clothes clean and mended. While it was still night, she rose to pack my dad's lunch and make his breakfast, then see him off for another long shift. After he drove away into the dark, she crawled back into bed and I snuck in beside her, taking my dad's place, rubbing my bare feet along her stubbly calves until I fell asleep.

Like that virtuous woman, she even sought out wool and flax—or at least the wool. Afternoons, in the coolness of the basement, she worked through the black plastic garbage bag full of last year's wool, shorn off an old ewe. What was destined for the dump, my mother collected gladly. On the wire bristles of one of her carding brushes, she set a clump of dirt-specked wool, and with the other wood-handled brush, dragged the fibres across the bristles. The ball of wool untangled into wisps. With each brush, the wool loosened and lifted from the bottom carding brush to the top one. The grit, bugs, and flecks of sawdust fell away until a tiny cirrus puff rested on her aproned lap. When she dropped it into the stainless-steel washtub, it seemed to hover a moment, floating on the furnace's draft. If, on a breezeless early-autumn afternoon, the sun was high and hot enough, she filled the washtub with warm water, and with a sliver of soap whittled from a block passed down through the family—soap that smelled of tallow and lye, ashes and birch trees—she scrubbed each fleecy cloud. Wet and washed, the wool perfumed the air with its animal history. Wrung out, it hung limp. But laid out on a faded bedsheet on the grass, the wool bleached white in the light until the back lawn looked like a pasture haunted by the ghosts of sheep.

Every night, before she tucked me and my brother beneath quilts filled with that wool, she sat on the bed, wedged between our pajama-clad bodies, and read aloud to us in a voice that rose and fell with the story's tension. When she read from *Little House in the Big Woods*, I wanted to be Laura Ingalls, to live inside the one-room cabin in the Wisconsin woods, to hear the wolves howl at night and have a bulldog named Jack that turned three times before settling by the fire to sleep, to have a Pa that played the fiddle as the blizzard winds blew. When she read *Heidi*, I dreamed a ladder to an attic bedroom and the mountain at my back, bluebells and alpine flowers, the crisp, clear air and goat-Peter singing down the trail to the village. When she read us all the way to Narnia, to Aslan tied down on the stone table and his mane shorn away, I bit the inside of my cheek until I lay in the dark alone, then sobbed into my pillow, not yet knowing how the story would end. When she read from *Uncle Arthur* of the mother who ran back into her burning house to save her sleeping baby, and of how in the morning the firemen found the two in each other's arms, burned to death, I imagined myself curled in my fiery bedroom, lying on the beige shag rug lit with sparks, and could see her crawling through the hallway dripping with flames, calling my name through the smoke.

I believed she was strong enough to save me from any danger. When she hoisted the axe above her head and cracked it down on a block of wood, those rounds of pine and fir split easily, over and over, in halves, then quarters, then cleaved to eighths. *Show us your muscles*, my brother and I would say. She shooed us away, told us to haul what she'd split, but we kept begging, *please, just show us*, until finally, she lifted one sleeve and flexed, her bicep a white bulge threaded with turquoise. And when we called her Popeye, she tugged the shirtsleeve down, shook her head and rolled her eyes, then picked up the axe and swung it down again.

43

Every time I called her name—*Mom, Mom*—the soft solo syllable, part hum, part cry, she appeared like magic. Every time I called—*Mom*—a miracle, a backlit shadow. When, in my bedroom, the mosquitoes whined and wheedled around my face, needling my sleep with blood-threat and itch, and from beneath the blankets I called *Mom*, she stood in her nightgown in the doorway, holding out the can of Raid. *Cover your head*, she said, and I ducked beneath the covers, burrowed down deep and sealed myself off from the aerosol hiss she sprayed above me, around me, across the whole room. She pulled the covers up to my chin. *Goodnight*, she said. *Sleep tight*, I said. *Don't let the bedbugs bite.* In call and response, we back-and-forthed the rhyme, and then she bent to recite with me our bedtime prayer—*Now I lay me down to sleep, I pray the Lord my soul to keep*—our voices moving quickly through the liturgy, its cadence as familiar as my mother's night-time smell of talcum and soap.

First god, woman above all other women, mother of all mothers, she was the one I reached for first inside the

Wednesday-morning huddle of praying ladies. Against my mother's warning, I'd gone roaming outside the sanctuary, had tried to pick a scruffy bouquet from the weeds in the ditch between the parking lot and road, but instead had come back with mud-crusted knees and white socks hooked with burrs. My quest for brighter fireweed and fatter rosehips had drawn me down toward the boggy culvert, and I'd fallen, twice, struggling up the slope of the ditch and back into the church. I tried not to cry, but as soon as the women looked at me, filthy and on the verge of tears, and their eyes went kind and their tongues clucked with compassion, I broke. I reached for my mother, and she reached for me, enfolding me into a perfume of Avon lotion and spearmint gum. The other women bent down around us and with a flurry of hands began to wipe away the mud from my knees, dabbing at the dirt and scrapes with tissues, plucking off the burrs stuck to my socks. While I cried into my mother's shoulder, they tended to me, murmuring a gentleness without words until my shuddered sobs calmed to breathing and they had removed the evidence of my fall. How far I'd strayed outside the boundaries, how shameful the filth, how worthless my now-wilted clutch of autumn weeds lying at my feet—these humiliations faded as I stood inside the circle of their low and soothing voices.

"Look," said Old Mrs. Wiens, pointing to my white socks. "All clean." She held open her handkerchief. Each Nettie, Sarah, Tina, and Ann poured in a handful of burrs. Old Mrs. Wiens tucked it in the pocket of her black cardigan and touched my cheek with her cool, blue-veined hand.

"Now," said my mother, licking her thumb to wipe dirt from my mouth, "let's go have something to eat."

The Bear's Dance

◇◇◇

EVERY MONDAY AFTER supper for three long years, I sat beside Mr. Everson, my hands resting in my lap, waiting for his first instruction.

"C-major scale. One octave, hands together."

I found my starting notes—right thumb on middle C, left pinkie eight notes below. Mr. Everson slid the weight of the metronome to an easy pace, unhooked the pendulum, and let it *tock, tock, tock* me into the scale's climb.

In the tiny one-level bungalow, his baby grand nearly filled the living room. The only other piece of furniture that fit was a small sofa tucked behind the piano bench, a place for other students to sit and wait their lesson turn. The piano, polished to a black sheen, looked like it belonged in the spiral-staircased, chandeliered home of a famous composer, not in these drafty, cramped quarters that smelled of burnt onion and dirty diaper.

On the other side of the pony wall, Mr. Everson's wife, dark-eyed, pale, and thin, except for her low, pouchy stomach, sat at the kitchen table in her bathrobe and slippers, her hair up in a towel. She spooned Pablum into their daughter's mouth and said nothing, not even to the baby, who, between bites, kicked her feet, slapped the high-chair tray, and squealed.

When I reached the octave's turn—left thumb, right pinkie—and started the descent, I felt it—my heart speeding up, bucking against the metronome's beat, anxious but trying to steady the notes, to keep my playing clean. *So far, so good, so far, so good.* The closer I came to ending in perfection, the more slippery my fingers on the keys. To make a mistake now would mean another week of practicing the same notes, the same song, because practice, said Mr. Everson, makes perfect.

Playing the week's pieces for him at my lesson stirred in me the same minor dread as when I stood in front of my teacher's desk to recite the monthly scripture memory passage. One stumble over a phrase—"Yea, though I speak with tongues of men and angels"—and Mr. Schmidt would correct, THE *tongues, and* OF *angels*, then tell me to practice the verses a few more times and try again tomorrow. One stumble over a run of dotted eighth notes, and Mr. Everson would lean forward over the page and with his sharpened pencil circle the shaky bars. In my music dictation book, he wrote directives for the coming week. *Count aloud. Staccato!*

Phrases—SMOOTH! Slow down. Speed up. Keep a steady, even rhythm as you play.

Praise from Mr. Everson came rarely, which made me crave it even more. For every half hour I spent plunking at the keys at home, my mother let me choose a marble from a jar in the cupboard above the stove, to add to my collection. But even without the incentive, I wanted to practice, to earn my teacher's nod of approval, his quietly spoken *Good work* or *Fine job* at the end of every song. I worked harder for him than I ever did for Miss Cindy, my first piano teacher, who during lessons wore fuzzy slippers and her hair in pigtails and said things like *Aren't eighth notes fun?* and *Wow, now that's fortissimo!* For every song I learned, Miss Cindy let me pick a sticker from a box. Scratch-and-sniffs, puffies, shinies— she had them all and gave them out as liberally as her praise. Even if I stumbled over notes in a simple one-line melody, she clapped her hands together, smiled, and said with a voice as bright as one of her glittery happy-face stickers, *I can hear you getting better every time you play!*

With Miss Cindy, I plodded through "Pony Ride," "Crack the Whip," "Turkey in the Straw," and all the other pieces in the primer level, adding stickers to my repertoire with every page we turned. Nothing needed to be perfect for Miss Cindy. Good enough was good enough for her. *Do your best, and let's move on*, was her philosophy. *New songs are waiting to be played!*

At the year-end recital, in the living room of her mobile home across from the hockey rink, after each student performed a final song to culminate the year of lessons, Miss

Cindy stood at the piano, faced us, and broke the news. She and her husband, Larry, were moving. She sniffled into a tissue, dabbed her eyes. He had a new job. She told us we were the best students she could have asked for. She wanted us to carry on with our music, to play for the sheer joy of it, and she'd help us all find a new teacher before she left.

"HE'S MORMON," MY mother said on the drive to our first lesson with Mr. Everson. "But don't say a word about it."

Her voice held the same low threat as when she whispered in church, *Don't stare at Mrs. Teichroeb*—the woman with the facial twitches who sat one row across from us. When my brother asked what makes a Mormon a Mormon, she told us that the women have a lot of babies, they don't drink coffee, and the men wear special underwear they can never take off.

"I don't understand it all," she said. "Just don't you dare ask about the underwear."

In the framed photograph that hung on his living room wall, he sat at a grand piano, dressed in a black tuxedo, the kind with tails. Near him on the massive stage, in front of a symphony orchestra, a conductor held a wand mid-air as if about to cast a spell over the rows of woodwinds, brass, and strings. Mr. Everson's hands hovered over the keys, ready to descend into the magic.

Why anyone like him would end up living here, said my mother, was beyond her. Like the other piano-lesson moms in town, she suspected his arrival here had something to do with him being Mormon. The running joke of the town was that you were either Mennonite or Mormon—or going to hell.

Maybe he was sent on a spiritual mission, or maybe our town was some sort of discipline doled out by the church, a city slicker banished to the six-month winter of a northern valley with a single traffic light.

While other men in town steel-toe-booted down our mud-splashed sidewalks in sawdust-covered lumberjack flannel and coveralls stained with engine oil, Mr. Everson wore dress shoes, slacks, and a crisp button-front shirt every day of the week. His brown hair parted neatly on the side, like a Lego figurine's. I never saw him pull a comb from his pocket and run it through his hair, yet no strand ever seemed out of place. The men I knew smelled like work, like lumber and grease and tailpipe exhaust, like cigarettes and coffee and beer. Mr. Everson, though, smelled like nothing in particular—an empty room, a piece of paper, an unscented bar of soap.

Everything about him was at odds with his surroundings. During the lesson, his snot-crusted baby in her saggy diaper pushed a chair across the kitchen linoleum, cruised the lesson area, crumpled any paper within her grasp, whined, cried, bellowed for attention. His wife stood at the stove warming a bottle, or sat at the table folding laundry, surrounded by stacks of dishes on the counter and toys on the floor. While his daughter gummed his kneecap, Mr. Everson, straight-backed in his teaching chair beside the piano, clapped out the rhythm I should follow.

When Mr. Everson chose a new song for me to learn, he always played it through so I could hear what it should sound like. He took the bench, I shifted to his chair. He clenched and unclenched his hands above the keyboard, drew in a deep breath, exhaled. He hovered his fingers a moment over the first notes, then leaned forward over the piano as he began.

No one I knew played piano like he did, with what he called "feeling" and "expression." At church, Aunt Mary and Cousin Betty and Cynthia Toews took their turns at the old upright Steinway, plugging away at the hymns as the congregation sang. Their chords trudged our four-part harmonies through verses and choruses of "Onward, Christian Soldiers" and "All Hail the Power," steady and solid as cinderblock brick.

Though his hands played the notes, his whole body seemed to play the song. He swayed. He arched. He listed. With his eyes closed, he tucked his chin down toward his chest. Then with his eyebrows raised, he tipped his face toward the ceiling. When the music lilted and skipped, a smile, sometimes a fluttering of the eyelids. When the melody warped to a minor dirge, a wince, a sadness on his face. His quiet notes fell featherlike, almost weightless, and his heavy double-*forte* chords, like a hammer on a nail, made me blink with every pound.

In the margins of my "Polonaise," he wrote, *More expression*. I didn't get it, didn't understand what he meant, let alone know what a polonaise was. Had I pictured a ballroom full of white-gloved men and festively gowned women dancing a grand Polish waltz, maybe my staccatos would have been as light as intricate footsteps over a marble floor, my phrasing as smooth as twirls and turns under stars. I might have imagined a lady and lord smooching beneath the moonlight while the music swelled. Instead, "polonaise" sounded to me like a gluey white paste, an old mayonnaise. My fingers got stuck in the sixteenth notes, and the three-four rhythm tripped me up.

At home, beneath the cool, bluish light of the piano lamp, I tried to play like he showed me—careful with the notes and counting out the rests, making each phrase a smooth, clean breath, but also playing with "feeling," with "expression." For every song, he wanted me to picture something in my mind when I played the notes. Every piece of music tells a story, he said.

When he played "Enchantment," he leaned forward into the keyboard. The *pianissimo* came delicate and soft from the hammers and strings. When the notes rushed forward, speeding up, he leaned back, swayed a little, then plunged back in with intensity.

"Do you hear it?" he asked.

I wanted to say yes. I wanted to say that I heard the story, that I saw it all in my mind as he played—the princess tip-toeing through the wind-swayed forest at night, the giant's footsteps stamping the frosty ground as he thundered after her. I wanted to hear the rush of notes like a gathering storm, a haunted castle, the princess taken captive, then her rescue, the knight's silver armour gleaming in the sun. But mostly, I heard the baby howling from her toppled stack of blocks and his tired-eyed wife clattering cutlery in the kitchen sink.

At home and seated at the piano in the corner of our living room, I opened my book to the song I'd been given: "The Bear's Dance." On the page, the quarter notes, the half notes, the dotted eighths and whole notes hung inside their clefs like code waiting to be deciphered. Black dots and empty circles, sharps and flats, phrase marks and numbers—they made me feel that I was missing something, that there was more behind the symbols to this locked-up world.

My fingers found the opening notes, staccato and minor. I tried rolling my shoulders like Mr. Everson did. I arched my back. I shut one eye. Nothing felt any different. I swayed side to side, but only a little for fear my brother might see me and laugh. I wanted my hands to pull from the wood and wire and ivory a bigger sound, a higher one, the kind that told the truth about the story in the song.

When the music dipped down into the bass clef, I felt a tilt in my gut, a sideways tipping toward something not right, like the telephone ringing in the dark house and the way my mother jumped from bed and ran down the hall to answer it. With its hinged lid open, the piano's sound was bright and loud. "The Bear's Dance" crashed against the walls as I crescendoed from *forte* to *fortissimo* and beat with fury the staccato chords.

Somewhere across the yard, my dad was making his way in darkness, a slow slog of boot-prints from the shop to the carport, trudging over gravel and the mulch of wet, dead leaves. When the door swung open, a draft of smoky night-cold would climb the stairs, whoosh a little gust of autumn grit around his feet, and he'd follow, one heavy step after another, like the weary whole notes that hung lonely in their clefs until the sober mood resolved and my dad stood inside the music at the threshold of the living room. The whirr of the microwave as my mother warmed his plate. Sparks popping behind the fire's mesh curtain, and at the hearth, my brother whittling a small block of pine into a boat, a car, a gun. My left hand slid an octave down to find the lowest quarter notes, and my right hand joined with bass-clef chords. The bear, following his hunger, his breath in ragged huffs, sour and musky, sniffed the air to smell what feast awaited. I kept thumping out the music, bar by bar, my hands trying to tell the truth about this beast lumbering under stars, part wild, part circus, dancing around the hunter's fire, paws dangling, shaggy feet pounding the earth.

Butchering Day

◇◇◇

T HE DAY ALWAYS started in darkness, and every man always brought his own knife. And always a gunshot cracked open the morning—then another. Two, three more shots.

I lay in bed, bracing for the squeal. When it came—and it always came, that shrill operatic rasping, unearthly, enough to churn the gut—I pulled the pillow over my head and hummed to block the noise until a final bullet dropped the screeching pig.

"Last one turned its head," Uncle John said later, laughing in his high-pitched stutter. "Yup. Got its ear pierced."

Light from the kitchen flickered beneath my bedroom door. The smell of *komst borscht*, a beefy cabbage soup, and the sound of my mother singing to the radio filtered in. At the back of the house, voices rose above the idling of engines—my uncles, my dad. When I stood on my bed and pulled back the curtains, my window lit up with headlights through the autumn fog. The shadow-shapes of men lurched from pigpen to truck as they lugged and loaded each dead hog.

Schwein schlachter happened every fall. Though our clan was not as Mennonite as most, we held on to certain customs and beliefs with a death grip—most of them having to do with God and food—and pig butchering was one of them. When morning frost began to cover the ground with a fore-shadowing of snow, and the season teetered toward winter, my dad and his five brothers marked a Saturday on their calendars, then announced it to their women, who spread the word to the rest of the extended family. *Come for Schweine-schlachten*, they said, *and bring your knives.*

SMOKE PLUMED A grey cloud above the roof of Great-Grandpa Martens's shed. Though the sun hadn't yet risen, cars and pickups already clogged the long gravel driveway. Aunts in kerchiefs and flannel jackets trundled boxes stuffed with thermoses of coffee and tea, pies, cookies, and squares. The cousins, my brother, and I, bleary-eyed but hyper with excitement, buzzed around the yard with rocks and sticks in our grip, little primitives waiting for blood. Through the trees, from their cabin at the back of the property, the old bachelor uncles came, jowly and carrying their knives.

In a lean-to connected to the shed, the men stood in a circle, passing around a whetstone. Each one spit on it, then drew his blade down and down again, scraping and sharpening until it gleamed. They stood beneath that lean-to for as long as they wanted, rubbing their thumbs slowly across the sharpened blades, talking in Low German—sounds familiar to me, but words I didn't understand. They smoked, talking trucks and bush camp, and drank their coffee, and when they were done, they snuffed their cigarettes and swigged their dregs, and the work began in earnest.

When they hefted the first pig into the scalding trough, and from a huge vat over the fire drew buckets of water to pour over the flesh, the smell that rose was like a mingling of smoked ham, rusted tin can, and outhouse sewage. As the steam cleared, the men hunkered in with their knives and began to scrape their blades across the skin to get rid of the hair and bristles. As soon as one pig was cleaned, they hoisted it up onto the long wooden table, and the next station of workers began their job of breaking down the carcass.

I loved to watch the pig being unzipped. Into the belly, right below the sternum, an uncle stuck the knife tip and dragged a slit clean down the torso. As innards oozed and bubbled up from the open seam of flesh, more hands set to work sorting the parts. In the doctrine of the butchering shed, everything that could be saved should be saved. What spilled from inside was a source of mystery and wonder. Here was death up close, and the mystery of what lay hidden inside a creature was gloriously on display, giving clues to the future I couldn't yet frame. When one of the knifed-open big-bellied sows spilled four tiny piglets, the uncles hollered for us to come and see.

"They look asleep, not dead," Aunt Agnes said when Uncle Corny pulled the piglets from the split-open sow, splayed on the table in the butchering shed. Everyone seemed a little sad and surprised.

With the other kids, I crowded around the table. Each piglet, small enough to curl in a Styrofoam cup, was perfectly formed, its hooves soft as new fingernails, the end of its snout like a button on a baby's sweater. In my hand, the piglet felt like a rubber toy, something the dog would drag to its bed and gnaw.

"It's a shame to just throw them away," my mother said, and so she slipped them in an old ice-cream bucket and set them in a cooler at the side of the shed. "We'll figure something out." Later, back at home, she'd pickle them in formaldehyde, two to a jar, their pink bodies snow-globed and floating in flecks of lifting light.

In the butchering shed, I peered over the table edge as the kidneys, liver, heart, spleen, stomach, and entrails were pulled from the pig, each warm, dripping organ named and held up for inspection—*healthy*, someone would pronounce, or *looks a little sick*—then either set aside in a bowl for use or tossed into a five-gallon oil bucket at the end of the table.

That bucket, full of the glibber and gristle and guts, was bound for the town dump, but until the uncles hauled it away, we kids were free to poke around in it. Like bargain-hunters at the discount bin, we jostled for spots at the rim, stabbing our sticks in as we fished for some glossy clot or slippery bit, then hoisted it close to each other's faces, saying, *Smell it, smell it!*

Of all the cast-off parts, I loved the bladder best. My mother washed it off in clean water, tied off the ureter with a double knot, and tossed it to me. The bladder, warm and wobbly, was the size of a football, but harder to hold on to. I tossed it to my brother, who set it on the ground and jumped on it. The bladder squirted out from beneath his feet but did not burst.

58

"Catch," he hollered, and threw the bladder back. I tried to grab it as it sailed toward me, but it slapped into my hands, slipped my grip, and blobbed to the dirt.

Kid to kid, we hurled the bladder as hard as we could huck it, in hopes it would splatter and spill its pee on someone. No luck. The bladder held, picking up dirt as it plopped, quivered, and rolled across the yard. We fell into loose teams, marked out boundaries, tried new ways of throwing and catching, and kept up our game of bladder ball, unaware that we were enacting the well-played game of our ancestors, or at least a version of it. To raid the rubbish heap and turn junk into some joyous thing was a creed that ran blood-deep. What child needs a china doll when she has a dried corncob wrapped in an old flannel diaper? Why beg for a BB gun when rock and stick will do? Who needs a pigskin when you have a brimming bladder? We played until the bladder landed near a grouchy uncle's feet. He bent down with his knife and slashed it, told us to go find some work to do. We crouched around the sack, watching it drain, pretending not to sniff the air above the puddle at our feet.

While the boys shadowed the men, who wielded the largest knives and blades and passed around a bottle of homemade wine to swig, I stayed with the women at the other end of the butchering shed. Everyone had a job to do. As the youngest female, I took up my post at the huge vat in the corner of the shed. The cast-iron cooker rested on a metal frame, inside of which a fire burned. Into the cooker, the aunts dumped cubes of fat, and as the fat melted and rendered down to lard, I stirred with a long wooden stick to keep it from burning. Every half hour, Grandma came by and dipped her finger in the white, greasy simmer, testing the temperature. Too hot and it will ruin the lard, she said. When it was nearly ready, Grandma dipped in her wire strainer and pulled off the cracklings, bits of pig skin separated from the fat and fried to a crisp. She ladled out the lard in stainless-steel tubs, and once it cooled, she poured it into syrup tins and coffee cans. At the bottom of the tubs of lard, the pig butter settled, to be scraped out into small plastic containers and divided at the end of the day. This was the *Schmaltz* my dad loved to spread thickly on a slice of white bread doused with salt and pepper, which he would then fry in a pan until crisp and smelling like bacon. He'd pour himself a tall glass of milk, sit down at the table, and with a fork and knife, cut the golden, toasted bread into small bites. Each forkful he dipped into an egg's runny yolk, then ate in silence, swigging milk every few mouthfuls, wiping the grease from his chin with the back of his hand.

After the lard was emptied from the vat, my dad came from the men's end of the shed, gripping the pig's head by the ears. He dropped it into the vat and covered it with water, then fitted the wooden lid on it, leaving it to simmer until the skin easily pulled away from the skull. Then, two uncles came to hoist it out with long forks. The pig's head, rising from the smoke and steam of the vat, brought every one of us kids close. The eyeballs had already been cut out and given to us to play with, our fingers working the stiffened lids and long lashes to make them blink like our own eyes. Now, the sockets stared back at me darkly. The mouth hung open in a loose smile. I'd see this head in dreams for years to come, an allusion I didn't know how to read, but one that merged with the face of every dead relative to become a ghost mask haunting me in sleep.

"And now we make headcheese," Grandma said, and pulled up a stool to the table. She bent her own kerchiefed, powdery face over the pig's head, her glasses steamed over from the heat. With her sharpened paring knife, she carved away every scrap and shred of fat and flesh, tooling away around the snout, collecting in a stainless-steel bowl every edible fleck found on that cooked skull. She'd mix the meat together with some of the hocks, adding salt, pepper, and spices, then let it set in pans like a jelly until firm and ready to slice.

WHILE THE MEN broke down the pig into chops, roasts, hams, and ribs, while the lard cooled and the headcheese rested, sausage preparation began. One at a time, the long, translucent intestines were drawn from the innards and brought to the women. Around the side of the shed, my mother and Mrs. Banman set up a washing station for the intestines. Mrs. Banman wasn't a blood relative but came to all our butchering days. At family gatherings and Sunday meals at my grandparents' house, right before we sat to eat, Mrs. Banman appeared at the back door in her kerchief and oversized coat, a look of worry always on her face. She has nothing, my mother explained, not even running water, not even a husband who's alive anymore.

Mrs. Banman came to work so that she could bring home meat at the end of the day. She was small and wiry and wore rubber boots, with long johns beneath her dark dress. Her thin face peeked out from a scarf tightly knotted under her chin. Her round glasses always seemed to be sliding down her nose. But she worked hard, her red, chapped hands flying to whatever task was given her. As Mrs. Banman held open one end of the intestine at chest-height, my mother poured a stream of warm lye water from a pitcher. My job was to hold the other end of the intestine away from the ground. As the liquid washed through, it pushed out whatever else was in the intestines. Out of the bottom end, into the dirt in a slosh at my feet, tapeworms slished and slithered in a yellowish tangle. When I prodded them with the toe of my boot, my mother warned, *Don't touch them, you'll get worms, too.*

After they washed the intestines, my mother and Mrs. Banman turned them inside out, then brought them in a bowl to the table where aunts with their paring knives scraped away the membranes, working down the length of each intestine to remove the pinkish tissue from the casing. The men, at their end of the shed, cleaned the knives and saws, hosed down the scalding trough, and set up the grinder. They stood over the butchering table and fed the scraps of fat and meat into the hopper. It oozed from the grinder's holes into a huge stainless-steel bowl. Grandma took charge of sprinkling in the salt and pepper, the brown sugar, then dug her bare hands into the meat and worked the seasoning through, turning and churning the mixture until it was a pinkish paste flecked with white, tasting bits of it as she mixed.

With the sausage nozzle attached to the grinder and the intestines washed and scraped and washed again, the sausage-making began. Grandma slipped a limp, thin intestine onto the nozzle, and the men took turns cranking the handle as Grandpa fed the ground-up meat back into the machine. As the meat oozed out to fill its casing, Grandma twisted the sausage into lengths, tying off the end and sliding on another intestine, the repeated motions of her hands like well-rehearsed choreography, sausage after sausage, until the grinder was empty.

What had been blood-streaked bits of a dead pig became something altogether new. The blood's iron tang had shifted to what smelled like food, our food, like the meal we'd share on Sunday, seated at the tables joined end to end to fit the whole family. When we all gathered around the butchering shed, it was like Christmas and a funeral, the togetherness and the feasting and the dead body close enough to touch.

After the scalding and scraping, gutting and cutting, cleaning and grinding, after the vat was scrubbed, all the meat cooled and wrapped in brown butcher paper and portioned out by family, after the smokehouse fire was lit and the meat hung, after the long wooden table had been washed and bleached and wiped dry, we gathered for a late-afternoon meal—*Faspa*.

Across from the butchering shed, on the other side of the dirt road, we shuffled into my great-grandparents' house. There, in Grosspa and Grossmama Martens' dining room, the women set out the food on long tables. Plates of cheeses. Pickles. Cold cut meats. Jams and jellies in glass jars. In a

porcelain mug, peanut butter and corn syrup stirred to a
sweet, gluey spread. Pots of soup—*zumma Borscht* with
smoked ham hock, green beans, carrots, potatoes, and sweet
cream, and *komst Borscht* with cabbage and beef—warmed
on the stove. And day-old homemade buns sliced and roasted
in a low oven until they turned to *zwieback*—that twice-
baked dark and golden toast hard enough to scrape the gums
when bitten.

As afternoon gave way to vesper hours, we gathered
around the table to share the meal. A bit of this, a bit of that—
for *Faspa*, whatever was on hand became the feast. While
in the shed the hams and sausages swung on their twine,
we stood together as Grandma Funk led us in the doxology,
our family's prayer for every meal—*Praise God from whom
all blessings flow*, we sang, *Praise Him all creatures here
below*—then sat and passed the plates around.

Grosspa sat frowning and jowly as a basset hound at the
head of the table, his white hair in horned-owl tufts. Beside
him, Grossmama countered with her soft, round face and
quiet smile, what few words she spoke coming out in Low
German. From them, my dad's family flowed. Down either
side of the table, aunts and uncles and cousins on stack stools
talked and laughed and ate. Toddlers and babies fussed and
chewed and banged the Formica with noisy cutlery. Tucked
in among us was the widow Mrs. Banman, hunched over her
soup, spooning it eagerly, wiping her nose with a paper nap-
kin between bites. The food didn't stop moving, always in
plates and bowls passed from hand to hand around the table,
the constant clink and clatter making a song of its own.

Above us, the heavenly host praised too, or so we sang. I pictured them as they were portrayed in the *Uncle Arthur* books—full-colour bright-blonde angels hovering above the green, green grass of Heaven. Around them, orchard trees glossed with plums, apples, pears. A blue, sparkling stream and sunlight beaming overhead like God's face shining in glory. And in the middle of it all, the banquet table overflowing with vast piles and platters of food—clusters of grapes, milk, bread, honey in the comb—like the all-you-can-eat Bonanza Steakhouse smorgasbord my father loved, but this one free and going on throughout eternity.

Below, at our meal's end, like voices cued in unison for a benediction hymn, my dad and his brothers loosened their false teeth, and with wooden toothpicks pulled from their chest pockets, picked at flecks and bits of gristle, tasting again the food we all had eaten, as the women rose from their seats, collected the dishes, and carried them back to the kitchen, dividing all the leftover food into containers, some for Mrs. Banman to take home, some for tomorrow's hunger.

After our feast and final cleanup, beneath a darkening sky with hardly a moon shining through, the butchering shed emptied, fire snuffed, lights out. Behind a skiff of dusky cloud, waiting in that other world of stars, the season's first snow hung, only days away from falling. We carried our haul of food to our cars and pickups, smoke and grease in our hair, the smells of the day woven into our clothing. My father and his brothers hollered in German back and forth across the yard, some joke about a pig, death, and a good sharp knife.

WINTER

WINTER

Target Practice

◇◇◇

N ONE MILKY Polaroid, we stand on the landing where the stairs split into two levels. At our back, the front door, and in the windows framing it, the winter dark from which we came. My brother wears a rubber mask over his whole head, turning him into a grey, straggle-haired man with a hooked, warty nose and missing teeth and eyes with soot-rubbed sockets. Beside him, I wear our dad's work boots and coat and his trucking company's blue ballcap, a pillow stuffed beneath my shirt to fatten me. Together, we're tramps come in from the cold. A minute earlier we were out on the porch, banging on the door until our mother answered, slurring our words, jeering and laughing at the joke we had become—two drunks on the road, begging for food, hollering, *Hey, lady, let us in.*

In another photograph, we sit side by side on the piano bench, our hands on the keys in duet form, my brother the bass, me the treble. No matter the hours we practiced, the song wouldn't come out right, his fingers, my fingers, stumbling over the shared notes. One slip on an accidental, one stuttered triplet, one tripping over the metronome's steady count and we devolved into fists and insults, the songbook tossed from the ledge, the lid slammed shut on someone's hands.

Though linked by blood, we were two creatures never meant to occupy the same close quarters—like the hamsters our dad decided should try sharing a house, for fun, to see if they might become friends. My brother and I had leaned on the fireplace hearth, watching our father lift Aunt Evelyn's hamster, the fluffy one we were looking after for the weekend, from its plastic dome, and slip it through the little door of the cage where Teddy, our own pet hamster, ran manically on his wire wheel. As soon as the guest rodent hit the wood shavings, Teddy, mid-jog, launched himself straight at his trespasser. The shrill, whistling screech that came from the cage made us all jump back. The two creatures, locked in a blur of white and gold fur, tremored and scrabbled and shrieked until our dad plunged his hand through the door and grabbed hold of one, which sank its tiny yellow teeth into his thumb. He yowled and dropped it on the living room rug, where it lay, bloody and with one eyeball hanging loose. We looked down at what had been Aunt Evelyn's fluffy hamster, now shredded and quivering. Back in his cage, Teddy panted frantically, his mouth and white chest fur streaked with red. "Well, that didn't go so good," said our dad. He scooped up the half-dead hamster from the rug and carried it down the stairs, out through the garage door, and into the darkness of the frozen yard so he could "take care of it." My brother and I pressed our faces to the kitchen window that overlooked the driveway, jostling for space on the countertop, elbowing each other, trying to see the end of the failed experiment.

We fought with a zeal reserved only for each other. And when we fought, we fought dirty. Wrestled on the carpet. Hurled curses. Pulled hair. He punched. I spit. He pummeled. I tattled. If his walloping fist didn't draw a bruise on my body, I made sure of proof. Holed up in my bedroom, I'd wham my own knuckles against the spot he'd punched until the skin purpled. With evidence of a wound, I slumped into the kitchen, eyes welling with newly brewed tears, and show off the bruise for sympathy and justice.

"But I didn't even hit her that hard!" my brother argued.

"Hard enough to bruise her," our mother said, and when she grounded him from TV for yet another day, I buried my smugness and smirk.

Manipulative, sneaky, tactical—that was my sisterly methodology. I plastic-wrapped his toilet bowl, squirted toothpaste on the seat. I spider-webbed a network of near-invisible thread throughout his bedroom, looping it around knobs, bedposts, through crotch holes of underwear folded in drawers. In the hallway outside his room, I flipped the clear plastic utility mat so that its toothy spikes poked up, and when he ran down the stairs toward his room, bare feet striking the sharp nubs, he screamed, hollered my name, the thorn in his flesh.

Brute force—that was my brother's style of warfare, along with the occasional verbal dart to bull's-eye my pride, but only until I plucked out the poisoned tip and dipped it in my own brand of venom, then fired it right back at him. If he called me *stupid*, I called him a *stupid jerk*. To his *lard-ass*, I threw back a *loser dork*. I savoured every insult as it formed, turning it over in my mouth like a hard candy, working the shape until it fit tightly inside my cheek. Each word was a shard that could cut, could draw blood if angled just so. As much as I hated having him sit on my chest and tap my sternum rapid-fire with his index finger in what he called "Chinese chest torture," I knew the pain would last only a finite amount of time, until either he tired of the torment or our mother walked into the room.

When my brother was angry, his eyes sparked wide, his jaw tensed, his teeth gritted. Fury narrowed my eyes, and I grew cool and sullen. If he was fire, I was ice. To my sun-white hair, pale eyes, and light skin, his dark hair, dark skin, dark eyes were the inverse, my shadowy foil. When he was a baby, strangers in store lineups and on sidewalks asked my mother if the father was Native, wanting to know if any tribal blood flowed from somewhere down the genetic line. Grandma Shenk sewed a fringed leather vest for him when he was a toddler and stitched him moccasins, too, which he wore with a headband made from a strip of leather and adorned with the feather of a crow. In the cowboys-versus-Indians story, he never wanted to play the cowboy. He wanted to wear the hides of animals and cook his bannock over an open fire, wanted to track and hunt and live wild in the woods. He ran face-first into the wind, leapt over fallen logs, fleet of foot. Behind him, I dragged my feet, dawdled, and whined about the miles. In a gang of boys, he was the quiet one, the sidekick and the shadow, not wanting the spotlight, never the bully. Clever, mischievous, fearless, tough, and fair, he was a boy I would have wanted as my friend—if he weren't my brother. Instead, I fitly filled the role of kid sister, earning well the names he levelled at me. *Pest. Turdface. Idiot. Bugger. Bag. Nimrod. Numbskull. Jerk.*

We could hardly be in the same room without turning on each other. At the supper table, when I threatened to cata-pult a spoonful of mashed potatoes his way, he glared and gave me his best Clint Eastwood: *Go ahead, make my day.* I let the starchy lump fly. A clot of white hung on his forehead a moment, then oozed down the bridge of his nose. His shock surged to anger. My bare foot, propped on an empty chair between us, caught his feral widened eye, and he stabbed it with the fork in his hand, hollering as he brought down the tines. Every road trip began with my mother dragging her index finger down the middle of the back seat. "Stay on your own side," she'd say, threatening with force, but a few miles into the trip, I'd already be edging closer to the line, seeing how far I might go before I lit the wick of his rage.

Only when we were alone together in the house did a measure of peace descend and civility reign. On those rare, parent-less, ceasefire evenings, we put aside the charley horses, purple nurples, door slamming, ear flicks, name call-ing, and stepped into the story we wished we always lived. My brother, my rival for power and territorial dominance, the one who ran faster through the trees, who could pop a wheelie on his bike without falling backward, whose pocketknife was always sharp, whose arrow and pellet and slingshot stone hit the mark when mine would not—in the empty house without a mom or dad to intervene, my brother became my ally, my defender, the one beside me, not against me. As the television fed us forbidden images—Agent 007 stroking the bare thigh of his lady-love, Rambo machine-gunning the jungle to a bloody spatter—we scarfed down whole bags of potato chips and guzzled pop straight from the bottle, all the while taking turns at the living room picture window, looking for any sign of our parents' return. If headlights started down the driveway, we'd shut off the TV, run to our bedrooms, dive under the covers, deep-breathing through the adrenaline rush, ready to feign sleep, and in the morning, keep our story straight: *No, we didn't stay up too late, and no, we never watched those R-rated movies.*

My brother and I didn't have a language yet for the deeper struggle, that unnamed turmoil beneath the skin of things. Time hadn't given us the distance and objectivity to see our lives clearly. When I stood guard at the night-time window, I had to press my face close to the glass to see into the darkness beyond my own reflection. Out there, in that other world, nothing was secure. Any tragic thing might happen. A car accident on the snowy road home from their evening out, a sudden brain tumour, lung cancer, heart attack, a fire that took them alive—the narratives played out in my mind and held me ransom to my brother's protection. If the two of us were left to fend for ourselves, then I needed him, and needed to love him. And wanted him to love me in return.

When mission bound us together, when the elements were against us, when in the sub-zero darkness I sat behind him on the Big Red, our three-wheeled all-terrain vehicle, and flew over snow and ice and slippery trails, my arms around his waist as we travelled his nightly newspaper-delivery route that seemed too many miles and too cold without my help, I felt the possibility of that love. When we arrived at the orange plastic box posted at the end of a driveway, I climbed off, stuffed in the rolled-up newspaper, and then hopped back on for the next leg of the journey. The wind, the noise of the motor, and the fat, padded helmets we wore kept us from speaking. No great sibling communion occurred in language. Snow flecked his goggles as he drove, but I closed my eyes and held on, the only time my arms around my brother felt justified, permissible, outside of a wrestling match or attempted escape from a headlock. If he felt any kinship with me, he never betrayed it, nor did I to him. After we delivered the final newspaper, he revved for home. When we hit a rut or bump, Big Red gained enough air to make my stomach lurch with laughter and my arms cinch tight around him, but the two of us said nothing to each other about the stunts. Still, our brief flight—that momentary hovering before we landed back on the snow-packed trail—held us together, brother and sister, bound, and flying through the ice and cold toward home.

If I could go back to him, I'd be a different sister, the kind who speaks aloud the buried love, who lets herself look up to her brother, no shame. If I could go back, I'd stand beside him in the clearing out back, behind the pig barn and the shop, and as he notched the arrow to the bow, I'd keep quiet,

73

crouched beside him in the snow, let him focus on the far-off target tacked to the frosty bale of hay. This sister—the one I wish I'd been—doesn't say *jinx*, doesn't bet two bucks he'll miss, and if he does—and the arrow flies off course, veers and arcs above the target—doesn't snark, *Nice job, great shot.* This sister prays the arrow straight, wills it through the drift of wind that threatens to undo its course, and bids it hit the true bull's-eye. And when it lands a mark, she throws her arms around his neck, unabashed, praises his shooter's eye and instinct. She runs toward the target so she can pluck the sunken arrow, bring it back, and say to him, *Now, let's do it again, this time even better than before.*

On Beauty

◇◇◇

CONSTELLATIONS IN A winter sky. The night road illuminated by snow. Beauty was above me, higher, thrum-
ming in the voltage of a storm and rising from the dirt
after a hot summer rain. In the birches and poplars flaming
with autumn, in the western sun's reddening over the field, in
the glitter of hoarfrost and the springtime drip of icicle thaw,
beauty named itself true. Whatever was beauty, was God.

Beauty was what made my mother stop in the garden at
twilight and point up at the moon, what made my dad snuff
his cigarette beneath his boot, hook his thumbs in his belt
loops, and shake his head in wonder. Beauty called, *Look up*.
When I lay on the dew-damp lawn with dusk settling deep
blue over me and counted points of light to find the Big Dipper
scooping darkness, beauty hushed and held me, breathed into
my lungs like back in the first beginning.

But everything was only a shadow of the one who made it. Stars, planets, the halo of the sun through cloud, snowflakes feathering down—that was beauty talking shop about its maker, the handiwork of a lofty God bidding the gaze upward in wonder. When we held open our dusty hymnals at Sunday service and sang, *Worship the Lord in the beauty of holiness*, I pictured angels with trumpets flying circles around a massive throne, jewels and gems the size of barn doors glinting in the smoke and mist, all the furniture of Heaven—gold streets, sea of glass, shining river, hovering seraphim and cherubim—opulent and royal and kitted out for paradise, pure by proximity to the perfect one.

Back on earth, in the eye of the beholder, beauty shifted definitions. Beauty was a word we didn't use often or well. It carried a heightened sense of the earthly. To be beautiful was to be otherworldly, to be different, to be *other*. The very sound of the word *beauty* mimicked birdsong—soft and taking flight on a cool breeze, disappearing into a high trill, then feathering into blue ether. To call someone beautiful was to set her apart from the gathered room, to usher her up a white staircase to a high balcony, to let her stand where every eye could see, while below, the rest of us gawked up in wonder.

THE ONLY WOMAN my mother ever called *beautiful* was the Sri Lankan lady who managed the drugstore cosmetics counter. In a town where most folks either bore Dutch or German blood, or descended from the Carrier-Sekani people, the make-up lady stood out as wholly different. With her turquoise and silver eyeshadow, black eyeliner that cat-eyed in the corners, and bright-pink blush streaking her high cheekbones, she seemed to have come from some exotic beyond. Her lips, lined and painted, formed a perfect fuch-sia bow. Beneath the fluorescent store lights, her long black hair, pulled back at the sides with jeweled barrettes, gleamed. When she rang through purchases at the till or waved goodbye to a customer, her gold wrist bangles jangled and shimmered.

"That woman is very beautiful," my mother whispered down to me as we passed a glass case full of expensive skin creams. "Look at her skin," she said. "It's flawless."

For my mother, beauty was carried from afar, tinted with mystery. The aurora borealis was beautiful. Miss Venezuela on the TV pageant show was beautiful. The Christmas music sung by the Mormon Tabernacle Choir was beautiful. On the album cover, the singers stood white-robed in tiers like layers of a living wedding cake. Through our stereo speakers, their harmonies poured forth something more celestial than the earthy four-part harmony of our Mennonite Sunday-morning hymns. "The Mormons believe that Heaven has seven layers," my mother said. "And they wear that secret underwear."

My dad's definition of beauty was tethered to a wholly other exoticism. To him, beauty was the funeral at which the deceased's younger brother gave a sobbing eulogy, and the open casket by which everyone paraded, sniffling into Kleenex, shaking their heads.

"Now that," my dad said, "was beautiful." He tapped his cigarette into the ashtray. "Looked like she was sleeping."

Beauty was brutal, came broken, was buried far too young.

To women, my dad never ascribed beauty. When he deemed a woman attractive, he used the term "good-looking." He favoured the types found crooning heartbreak on the stage of the Grand Ole Opry or leaning in a too-small bikini against a dripping-wet Kenworth. Tammy Wynette in her fringed Western denim—good-looking. The peppy new waitress at the Pine Country, hand cocked on her hip as she flirted with the breakfast regulars—good-looking. Daisy Duke lounging on the hood of the General Lee in short-short cut-offs and a plaid shirt tied into a halter—well, she was good-looking.

Whenever the TV flashed the latest country-music video by Tanya or Reba or Dolly, my dad said, "Now that's a good-looking woman."

On the wives of his trucker buddies, he weighed in freely. Shirley with the tight jeans and smoker's laugh, good-looking. Moon-faced Trudy, not so good-looking. Debbie, leather-skinned and shy, used to be good-looking, but the years have been cruel.

My mother, standing before the full-length mirror in her new flutter-sleeved black and teal dress, fluffing her perm for the Legion's New Year's Eve party, called the attention of my dad's gaze. He stood behind her, assessing.

"And how much did you have to pay for that?" he asked.

But he wouldn't say the word.

ON THE OUTSIDE wall of the shop, against the residue of yesterday's sun and the evening's woodstove heat, moths and butterflies congregated. Flattened against the warmth, their wings adorned the beige stucco with spots and scales, whorls and flecks. Every morning, my mother in gumboots and garden jacket hunted them, her hatpin aimed at the lit and resting insect, then the prick of the silver tip through the fuzzy thorax, and the pluck off the wall and into the empty jam jar.

79

At the kitchen counter, I watched her dip a cotton swab in rubbing alcohol and dot it on the creature's head. It flittered, flexed. Thread-legs trod the air until it withered to a still specimen. I knew the kill to be the dirty work of this pursuit, but unlike draping a chicken on the chopping block so we could eat its meat, the snuffing of the moths and butterflies gave us nothing, except the chance to gaze close-up at the feathery scales patterning their wings.

My mother displayed them on a slab of white Styrofoam and labelled each one with a name pulled from a guide to moths and butterflies of British Columbia. In neat blue ballpoint, she printed names like Tortoiseshell, White Admiral, Mourning Cloak, and Hoary Angelwings on tiny slips of paper, then sticky-taped each slip beneath the corresponding specimen. What once broke loose from a gauzy cocoon and flew who knows how many miles across forests and meadows and lakes and logging roads now lay pinned in uniform rows for eye-level wonder.

"Don't touch them," she said, "their wings are made of dust."

I WANTED TO be beautiful the way Joanie Olsen was beautiful. At the winter carnival, Joanie skated the spotlight number to the love theme from *Ice Castles*. I sat in the crowd hush of the darkened bleachers, fully mesmerized by her sparkle-skirted mini-dress, her feathered hair swooshing with every turn and pivot. Under the disco ball's starry shards of light, Joanie leapt, looped, and landed with her arms unfolding in silver-glittered wing-sleeves. As she spun in camel position at the centre of the rink and the soundtrack string section swelled through the P.A., cameras flashed among the rows of spectators, and I saw what I didn't have.

I knew I wasn't beautiful, not in the way the world gauged and praised. Too many times, I'd stood beside a female cousin or schoolmate at a bathroom mirror or in a window's reflection and witnessed our differences. My blue-grey eyes, chubby face, and snub nose did not compare to the dark and delicate features of the girls around me, the ones who garnered breathy *wows* and admiration for their shiny, naturally curly hair, rosebud lips, and eyes like chocolate drops. They looked like the girls who glossed the pages of catalogues and sales flyers.

At a medical check-up, a new resident doctor looked with concern at my white-blonde hair and pale skin and asked my mother if I might by any chance be albino. Back at home, I slid volume one of the encyclopèdia off the shelf. Under *Albino*, I read words like *pigment* and *photophobia* and *mutation*. I learned that albino animals rarely survive in the wild, that the sun burns their skin to cancer. A picture of a white-haired, white-skinned girl stared back at me from the page, her eyelashes and brows bright white—even whiter than mine. She looked as if she'd been dipped in winter, abandoned to the ice and snow.

SPEND TEN MINUTES every day, my grandmother urged me, pushing the two front teeth together. "It'll lessen the gap a bit," she said. "But small teeth run in the family, so you'll never have a perfect smile."

"Now pinch your cheeks and count," she said. I gripped the flesh fat between forefinger and thumb and squeezed.

"And bite your lips," she said, "a little on the top, a little on the bottom." I pressed my bottom teeth against my upper lip, then switched to top teeth, bottom lip, back and forth.

"Count to thirty," she said, and I obeyed.

When I released my grip and relaxed my lips, Grandma held a pocket mirror up to my face. "See that extra colour?" she said. "That's natural cosmetics."

Alone in my bedroom, in front of my dresser mirror, I practiced ways of smiling that would hide my teeth. I bit my lips. I pinched my cheeks. I watched the brightness swell.

"CHARM IS DECEPTIVE, and beauty is fleeting; but a woman who fears the Lord is to be praised," said the book of Proverbs. Your beauty, said every pastor, every preacher, every prophet, comes from within. The Lord looks at the heart, not at your outward appearance.

In the Sears catalogue, the girls smiled with blushing cheeks, straight white teeth, and lips tinted with gloss. Their bangs curled under with a little puff above their arched eyebrows. Above my nearly white brows, my bangs fell jaggedly, despite my mother's *Family Circle* magazine cost-saving tip for cutting bangs straight. While I perched on a stack stool, she fastened a strip of Scotch tape across the bottom edge of my bangs. With one drawn-out slice of the sewing scissors, she cut away the sticky strip together with the stuck-on hair, and then chucked it in the garbage can beside the toilet.

82
As young girls, my mother and her sisters plucked blossoms from a rose bush and tucked the red petals between their lips. When their father caught them vaunting around the house on tiptoes, pretending to be high-heeled and lipsticked society ladies, he scolded them with the story of Queen Jezebel, a painted woman who grew so vain from looking at herself in a mirror all day that she fell out a window and died, her blood licked up by dogs.

When God looked deep down in my heart, he surely saw me·posing like her in my polished mirror. He knew the dark knot in me, how badly I wanted someone to say, "Look—do you see that girl? Her white hair, the way it catches sunlight? Her eyes, like sky and river slate flecked together? Look at her. Just look at her."

AFTER SUPPER, WHILE the adults played cards at the Nicholsons' dining room table, I snuck back into the guest bathroom and turned on the sink faucet. I checked the door again to make sure it was locked. I let the water run to mask the sound of me sliding drawers and opening cupboard doors. At home, my mother's vanity held Avon face cream in a plastic green tub, a tube of pale beige cover-up for dark circles beneath her eyes, and a bottle of amber perfume called Tabu.

But here, on the bottom shelf of Mrs. Nicholson's medicine cabinet, lipstick tubes stood in a neat row. I heard the small voice whisper, *Don't*, but still I lifted a tube of lipstick, careful and with a steady hand so that I wouldn't domino the others. I uncapped it and swivelled the base. A nub of sunset rose. I chose another tube, then another and another, until the countertop bloomed an array of reds, pinks, oranges, and mauves, like all the richest crayons in the box. One by one, I lifted the colours. I watched in the mirror as my puckered mouth changed from coral to poppy to ruby to plum.

With each new colour I applied, the lipstick picked up the hue left behind, and each tube now bore traces of the one before it. Dark violet, now smeared with rust, had lost its voltage. What had been dusty rose looked more like dirty brick.

"Are you okay in there, honey?" Mrs. Nicholson, outside the door, called to me.

I flushed the toilet. I turned the taps off, then on again. "Just about finished."

As I rushed to swivel down and cap the lipsticks, some tubes clattered to the floor. I coughed. Flushed again. Listened for the voice outside the door. I lined the lipsticks up in a row on the lowest cabinet shelf, but I couldn't make them straight.

In the mirror, my lips, now layered with eleven swipes of colour, had darkened to a waxy bruise. Even after I wiped my mouth with a wad of dampened toilet paper, scrubbed with a bar of hand soap, I still wore the proof. The Jezebel spirit, like Grandpa warned so many years ago, had found a willing vessel.

"GLORY TO GOD in the highest!" proclaimed an angel harnessed in cardboard wings and haloed with silver garland. "And on earth, peace! Goodwill toward men!"

The pianist arpeggioed our carol's opening chords, and Mrs. Penner, perched on the front pew, lifted her hands to count us in. In the front row of the Sunday-school children's choir, pinned by the brightness beaming from the balcony, I stood in my Christmas dress, blue calico with a velvet bodice and dark-blue lace at the cuffs, the one my mother had sewn for me.

Evenings, after supper, I'd stood on the brown, padded seat of her sewing chair and turned a slow circle as she pinned the hem in place, the pinpoints snagging and pricking the skin below my knees. I felt important, like royalty on a pedestal. The pleats and darts, the shoulder puffs and sweetheart waist—my mother altered them to my shape so that when I wore the garment, it fit me perfectly.

Zipped into that dress, I wanted to be good, to kiss my mother's cheek, to not jab my brother when he crossed the invisible line dividing our territory in the car's back seat as we drove across the bridge toward the church, to let my dad hold my hand as we walked into the sanctuary. In that dress, I felt like beauty might soak through to the inside of me and turn me pure.

My father's eye was on me. I was sure. In some hard wooden pew, he sat at the back of the sanctuary, watching me, me in my blue dress with the shiny ribbons cinched tight across my rib cage and tied into a bow. Beside me, behind me, other flush-cheeked girls in their own dresses sparkled and swayed, their hair preened in barrettes and bows. My own hair, curled and combed by my mother's deft hand, shone white under the spotlight. *Close your eyes and hold your breath*, she'd said, then sprayed my head with an aerosol mist that smelled like perfume and disinfectant. *This will hold it all in place.*

Like a pageant hopeful, I smiled into the darkness and opened my mouth, ready to lift the long open *O* of "O Holy Night" into the rafters. I wanted the tune to splinter through the roof, up, and up, for it to glide into the heavens and float all the way to Jesus's feet, where it would land like flowers, myrrh, and incense, like the beauty and splendour of holiness. Inside the choir's swell and swarm of voices, my song flew up, a speck of glitter, a dust-winged thing, a fleck of light in falter, straining to become a star.

The Carol Sing

◇◇◇

COME DECEMBER, YOU'D see the signs everywhere, taped to the steamed-up glass of Woody's Bakery, bold-lettered on the door of Taylor Brothers Hardware, papering the windows of Diamond Jim's Video, Jewelry, Used Books and Pellet Stoves. *Come one, come all*, proclaimed the posters tacked on telephone poles and storefronts. *Come one, come all to the Community Carol Sing!*

This was one of the nights when the whole town gathered, a ritual on our municipal calendar, announced weeks in advance on the front page of *The Omineca Express-Bugle* alongside advertisements for "Midnight Madness," Vanderhoof's holiday spending spree, where all the stores stayed open until the stroke of twelve, sidewalks bustled with people scrabbling for bargains, and Aunt Evelyn seemed always to be careening around a snowy corner in her van, hollering the hourly surprise specials—*Co-op's got butter for a dollar a pound!*—to my mother, whose hand I gripped as we navigated the steady flow of shoppers.

Our town's social life followed the rhythm of the seasons, each shift in weather signalling a reason to come together— the summer air show, the fall fair and rodeo, the greasy carnival that rolled into town every spring on dusty lowbeds and set up in the empty lot across from the bowling alley. In a town our size, small in population but sprawled out over miles, any event was cause enough to make the drive into the valley, to close the rural distance between houses, the wide acres of pasture and forest that separated neighbours.

But the Community Carol Sing, our winter tradition, held a feeling that set it apart from the town's other events. Every element—the darkness, the cold, the streets and buildings strung with lights—tilted the world away from the ordinary and toward the miraculous. From across the tracks and both sides of the frozen river, traffic rumbled over the roads and down into the valley, a northern caravan of exhaust fumes winding toward the local high school. Into the gymnasium we tromped, hundreds of us in heavy coats and boots, snow melting into puddles where we trod. The gym that usually reverbed with cheers, sneaker-squeak, and the thud of a bouncing basketball now lay in darkness except for a few flickering overhead fluorescents and the blinking strings of coloured lights strung up along the walls, hoops, and scoreboards.

As we bustled and climbed into the rolled-out bleachers, the crowd's small-town small talk buzzed in the wide-open room—gruff discussion of the cold snap moving through, who bought the old Schultz farm off Braeside Road, whose dog bit whom and why and how, and what to do about the falling price of lumber.

Jammed shoulder to shoulder, our crowd was the town's true cross-section: loggers and cops, accountants and hair-dressers, seniors from the care home and runny-nosed kids sweating in their snowsuits. In one huge room, the stoic Lutherans and turtlenecked Anglicans, the equally repro-ductive Mormons and Mennonites, the wild Pentecostals and rosaried Sisters of St. Joseph (*Don't stare at the nuns,* my mother whispered)—we all came together, ready to sing.

I'd been raised in communal song, surrounded by the voices of the congregation at the Evangelical Mennonite Church, the men dipping down into the low bass or holding the reedy tenor, the women wavering on the soprano melody or skimming steadily below it in the alto tones. When I stood beside my mother in the pew, holding one corner of the heavy open hymnal and following her lead, the music enfolded me so that I became a swaddled thing within it. But gathering on Sunday for a church service and plodding through a hymn with the voices I knew well, many of them belonging to fam-ily, was different. To be one in a crowd of people who were familiar but still mysterious, to share a bleacher seat with the tall, curly-haired woman from the produce section at the Co-op grocery store, or to spot, one row up, the man with the goiter, that turnip-sized, purplish bulge on the side of his neck—to breathe alongside these almost-neighbours, almost-strangers made the occasion seem magical, like a scene in a dream where my earthbound body, cut loose from the law of gravity, suddenly took flight.

WHEN THE SPOTLIGHT rose on the low podium, and the high-school band lifted their instruments, and when the music teacher raised his baton, we rose, too, as the opening bars of "Deck the Halls" drummed and trumpeted us in. And we sang, our voices surging at every *fa-la-la*, hushing into "O Little Town of Bethlehem," then vaulting back up into "Jingle Bell Rock." To the right, my first-grade teacher and her stern-browed husband. To my left, a row of fidgety cousins, an aunt, an uncle. And leaning in the doorway, some of the Stoney Creek men who stood on the corner by the Reo Theatre and sometimes called me *Blondie* when I passed. Together, we belted it out, one raucous choir breaking into four-part harmony whenever the choruses came around, then returning to the simple, unified melody of the verses.

But the true high note of the evening always came near the end, when the town's barber, John Zandbergen, made his way to the microphone. Even as a kid, I felt the thrill of that moment when the spotlight brightened on him. Though I'm sure he must have worn a suit jacket and slacks, in my mind he was wearing his white barber's smock, high-collared and button-snapped. His chest pocket held no pocket square, but a pair of silver scissors. His dull brown hair and wide mustache gleamed in the light. When the speakers swelled with the canned orchestral backing track, he lifted his hands to his mouth, leaned into the microphone, and began to whistle.

What song he whistled, I don't recall. But how he whistled—that was unlike anything I'd ever heard. His breath took the melody and flew it upward, lilting, spiralling as if on wings, a pirouette, a twirl, a whirling silver trill that rose and dipped like some strange bird sprung loose from its winter cage and freed into the sun. John Zandbergen—the town barber!—whistled that gymnasium into wonder—the nuns, the fussing babies, the mayor and his council, the truckers and trustees and housewives and ranchers—all of us. His hands fluttered at his face, trembling the tune, soaring it, unscrolling it, flying it lofty and alight, then winging it down to rest in a clear held note that faded into silence.

We rose to our feet. We clapped and clapped for this man, the town barber, this ordinary human whose whistling made anything seem possible. If that song could rise from a man who daily razored the stubbled jawlines of cussing truck drivers, who buzz-cut every fidgeting farm boy in town and trimmed the wild eyebrows of old men, if by some strange miracle his song could rise like that, then so could anyone's.

The Community Carol Sing closed with a final rousing stand-to-your-feet and sing-as-you-leave song. As we made our way back to the parking lot in a collective shuffling of boots through snow, more than one man, low beneath his breath, whistled as he walked to his pickup truck, picking up the song still playing inside. The breath of all that whistling scrawled the air with a little rush of warmth, the winter night bending to the lowly tune beneath a sky heralding stars to guide us along the icy road for home.

Gloria

◇◇◇

EVERYONE WAS AN angel at first. We started off the same, floating amorphous in bleached-out bedsheets every December for the school Christmas musical. I blurred, like all the others, into the chorus of white robes. When the piano played the opening chords, I sucked in breath and filled my lungs to belt out hallelujah with the other voices, one anonymous angel singing with the host.

I was happy at first to be counted in the choir, to join the melody that travelled up and ever up toward the finale's whole note, held to draw applause. Though my twisted-pipe-cleaner halo scratched my scalp and made it itch, at least I had a halo, silvery and sparkling. At least I didn't have to be a shepherd with a tea towel on my head, carrying a broom-stick for a staff. Sure, the audience laughed at the shepherds as they bumbled in their bathrobes up the side steps of the stage while shielding their eyes from our angelic splendour. Sure, the three wise men got to carry their moms' jewelry boxes and empty perfume bottles to the manger-side, kneel in reverence, and touch their foreheads to the floor in worship. Wedged between my fellow nameless angels, I was just another bedsheet on the line, content to blend in with the laundry, at least the first few times around.

But I saw the way that spotlight hit the stars, those kids with speaking roles who stood downstage inside an illuminated circle and spoke their lines, sang their solo parts above our choir's background *ooh*s and *aah*s. I wanted what they had, that moment bathed in full attention, all audience eyes on me. I wanted to be singled out, noticed by the crowd. I wanted what Gloria Dick had won—the leading role with all the monologues and solos—but every year she earned it with her pure and sweet soprano, her thin white wrists, her glossy brown hair, her cocker-spaniel eyes.

If Gloria was the polished flute, I was the oboe with a split and rasping reed. I could carry a tune but had to jut out my chin and strain to hit the high notes. I had no trouble memorizing lines but somehow couldn't bend my voice to do what it needed to make Miss Hornsby, the music and drama teacher, choose me. When Miss Hornsby asked who'd like to try for the lead, I always raised my hand high, stayed quiet, smiled as righteously as I could without looking proud, my eyes bright and blinking a signal as I swirled a prayer inside my heart and head that whispered to the chapel ceiling, *Pick me, pick me, pick me.*

In one nativity, Gloria was Mary in a blue-and-white gown sewn by her mother, kneeling beside Rocky Peters, a red-faced

Joseph. She stared into the straw-filled manger as if the swaddled baby truly was the Messiah and not an old doll swiped from the church nursery. For the play about the animals in the Bethlehem stable, Gloria was the little lamb offering her whole fleecy self to the holy family, foreshadowing the Christ child as the perfect lamb who takes away the sins of the world. While she sang her meek solo in a white woolly cape and lamb's-eared hat, I stood in the background mooing softly, wearing a cloth hood with plush horns sewn askew. 93

When Miss Hornsby announced a new Christmas musical about a team of angels working to get the latest campaign off the ground and into the sky over Bethlehem, no one was surprised that Gloria won that lead, too. As Carol Angel, she busied herself with Heaven's housekeeping and choir practice and trumpet polishing. During rehearsals, when Gloria gave her monologue and Miss Hornsby asked for more excitement, more volume, more energy, I stood at the back of the stage with the rest of the supporting angels and ran her lines in my head, pictured myself in Gloria's place raising my hands like a healing evangelist, proclaiming the good news like a real archangel, one so genuine and holy and with such vivid blonde hair, it was hard to tell that I wasn't the real celestial thing.

Whether Miss Hornsby watched me mouthing Gloria's lines during practice or simply needed a failsafe, I don't know, but after one of the rehearsals, she pulled me aside and handed me a stapled script with my name pencilled at the top.

"If you like, you can be the understudy," Miss Hornsby said. "Learn Gloria's part, and if she gets sick, you'll fill the role. It's a big responsibility."

That night, in my bedroom, in front of my mirror, I practiced all of Carol Angel's lines and movements. With a hand above my brow, I peered at Earth below. I threw my hands up in frustration at the absentminded angel, sighed with exasperation at the progress of the choir, crossed my arms, smiled, winked, practicing what it meant to be a good angel, the best angel ever, all the while wishing fallen-angel wishes—that Gloria would be struck with the flu or mumps or leprosy.

The day before the big performance, during final rehearsal, Gloria, crowned in gold garland, floated in her fluttery white dress, expressive and spritely, while I hunched in my requisite white sheet, waiting for her to make a mistake. On one side of me, Teddy Dueck stuffed his hand into the neck hole of his shirt and levered a sweaty fart from his armpit when Miss Hornsby wasn't watching. On the other side, Tammie, who smelled like old underwear, breathed hard through her mouth.

"We bring you good news, grrrrreat news!" Gloria proclaimed, throwing her arms wide open to the empty pews that soon would fill with her admirers.

More than anything, I wanted to proclaim the bad news about Gloria: that once, in chapel service, I'd seen her blow her nose, peek into her Kleenex, and then covertly peel the snot from the tissue with her front teeth like a cat pulling flecks from a fishbone. But I didn't know how to say to Miss Hornsby—without seeming like a jealous snitch—that the wide-open mouth singing the rising holy notes was the same mouth that chewed mucus chunks when we bowed our heads for chapel prayer.

On the shadow edges of the limelight, I lamented my understudy status, convinced I was meant for a more dazzled life. If God's eye was on the sparrow, like the hymn proclaimed, then surely God's eye was on me, too. The psalms said that he numbered the hairs on my head, knew when I slept and when I woke, was spying on me always like a mom. I wanted to believe that he saw me as more than a wingless no-name, but my place in the back row confirmed a more minor identity: less the star and more a drifting dust mote, caught briefly by the beam, then gone.

ON THE NIGHT of the performance I arrived one hour early and joined the buzz of hyperactive angels milling around the basement classroom, donning our costumes and receiving final directions from Miss Hornsby, who ran us through our musical cues. We were a choir ready to belt out the hallelujahs and recite in chorus the Gospel of Luke in which Quirinius was governor and Caesar Augustus issued a decree for a census—all words that made little sense to me, but that sounded ancient and important. Miss Hornsby kept checking the door, peering out into the parking lot.

"Has anyone seen Gloria?" she said, scanning the room with nervous eyes.

What felt like a tiny spark lit in my gut. She wasn't here. No one had seen her arrive. That spark sizzled and threatened to crack into fire. Miss Hornsby kicked into action, sending searchers into the parking lot, the foyer, the sanctuary. She stood inside the staff room with the telephone receiver to her ear, dialing numbers, but nothing. No answer.

At five minutes to showtime, with every angel lined up and ready to shuffle up the stairs and onto the church stage, Miss Hornsby tapped me on the shoulder and called me aside. In a corner of the classroom, she held me by the shoulders and said, "Do you know Gloria's lines?"

I nodded my yes, vigorously, dramatically, and nearly added an "amen." In my mind's eye, I already saw myself on stage as Carol Angel, zipped into the flutter-sleeved white dress fitted for Gloria.

"Can you sing the final song?"

Again, I nodded. Miss Hornsby had no clue how many times I'd practiced alone in my bedroom, my dresser mirror the audience to which I made my face go solemn and holy, mimicking the dreamy Heaven eyes and slightly tilted head of the angel that hovered over baby Jesus in the *Children's Picture Bible.* I could be that angel, sinless and pure, proclaiming the arrival of a new, surprising greatness.

At seven o'clock, the sanctuary dimmed and I took my place on stage. Instead of standing in my usual row, I stepped forward, and waited for the light to fall. I looked out into the pews, all of them filled with people made unrecognizable by the darkness. Somewhere, among the other moms and dads, my mother perched on the edge of her seat with a camera in her lap, ready to aim her flashbulb when I appeared, still thinking that I was one of the choir's nameless. As the pianist played the opening bars of the overture, and all the angels watched Miss Hornsby's hand conducting us toward our first notes, I saw at the back of the church a girl in silhouette being hurried along by a woman.

It was Gloria, shuffling with her mother through the packed sanctuary, trying to get to the stage to take her place, but the music was telling her she was too late, and her mother was tucking an arm around her shoulder, drawing her back, pulling her close. At the end of the centre aisle, against the back wall of the church, Gloria turned her face into the crook of her mother's coat sleeve, as if she might be crying. Then as the spotlight dawned on me, she disappeared with all the other faces into darkness.

Throughout the play, Miss Hornsby crouched in the front pew with a script on her lap, ready to cue me, but I knew the lines, hit my marks, spoke the monologue—*But the innkeeper won't give them a room! Where will Jesus be born? Where? Where?*—with as much feeling as I could muster. When the audience laughed, I took it like a gold star and stuck it in my heart.

When it came time for my solo verse in the play's closing number, I moved downstage and stepped into the light that beamed down from the ceiling. The aisle stretched in front of me, and at the end of it, the shape of Gloria still clinging to her mother's arm. She could have marched on stage, nudged me aside, and taken back her Carol Angel costume, could have made me fade into the background where I began, belonged. And I could have offered to stand aside and let the stage lights throw their gold over her freshly combed and curled hair. Instead, I held my ground, my solo's spotlight place, and sang my lines, clear and bright: *O come to my heart, Lord Jesus, there is room in my heart for Thee.*

Even as I sang, I knew the truth of it. No room, I thought.

Not in the spotlight's beam, not on the stage decorated like Heaven, a twinkling miracle, tinselled and spangled with glitter. No room for Gloria, and if no room for her, then surely no room for the baby Jesus born in Bethlehem. No room for anyone but me and all my starry dreams.

As the song ended, just like I'd practiced in my bedroom, I hinged forward at the waist, one arm crossed in front of me and the other tucked back, knees slightly bent. In the brightness of the spotlight, I bowed, my shadow thrown behind, my hair shining whitely, every flyaway strand lit up, numbered, and known.

Christmas Eve, Loop Road

◇◇◇

WE ATE THE same meal every Christmas Eve: clam chowder, homemade buns, pickles, and a salad made with orange Jell-O, canned mandarins, Cool Whip, and cottage cheese. All day, my mother stirred the pot steaming on the stove, punched down dough, shaped the rolls. The living room's tinselled jack pine perfumed the house. The radio gave updates on Santa's whereabouts, and though neither my brother nor I had ever been allowed to believe that a fat man in a flying sleigh sailed the globe and dumped presents down chimneys, we both felt the anticipation rising in the countdown hours toward morning and our own pile of gifts beneath the tree.

Dusk slid into darkness down our rural road, leaving only the snow to lighten the sky over us. The picture window mirrored back our family scene: my brother and me on the rug raking through a pile of Lego, the TV glowing holiday cartoons, and beyond us, the table, set for supper.

We were waiting for my dad to show up. Already, Mom had phoned around to some of the usual places—Sparky's, Clem's, and Striegler's shop, searching out my dad to call him home. We were, it seemed, always waiting for him, always asking when, how long, how many more lines on the clock face before he pulled into the driveway. My mother clicked down on the receiver, then dialed another number.

"I'm looking for Football," she said.

No matter how many times I asked, my dad refused to tell me why his friends called him that. Football. He didn't play the sport, didn't do anything athletic, except pitch a game of horseshoes now and then at summer barbecues, or shoot snooker at his father's billiards table. I guessed that the nickname might have something to do with the tune that we sang along to on his pickup stereo, the song that went, "Could've been the whiskey, might've been the gin" and then the line about the singer's head feeling like a football the morning after the party.

"Supper's waiting," my mother said into the phone, her voice a taut wire. On the other end, amid laughter and the buzz of men's voices, he'd tell her he was coming, don't get so hyper, the card game was almost done, he was just finishing his drink, he'd be home soon.

Though his evening lateness had become commonplace, we kept checking the window for headlights. Always, the question hovered: *What if he doesn't come home?* On

Christmas Eve, the threat level seemed higher, with more at stake. No Dad, no Christmas. No Christmas, no gifts. When lights slowed on the road out front and turned up the driveway, my brother and I, on our knees on the sofa, heralded his arrival with *he's here, he's here, Dad's finally here.*

He took his time coming in from the yard. He must have sat in the pickup a moment, drawing in the final puffs of his cigarette, tapping the ash in the pullout tray, clicking off the radio's country carols. What he thought about as he walked across the yard from his truck to the carport, I never wondered. I only waited for the sound of his hand on the doorknob, the stamp of snow from his boots on the front step. Then the door swung open and a little blizzard of cold wind rushed up the staircase and into the dining room, where we sat at the table with his empty chair at the head.

After the usual back-and-forth between them—my mother telling him to wash his hands, my dad arguing they were clean, clean enough, and finally, the compromise of a soapy dishrag to wipe off the grit and grease—he eased down into his seat with a groan. My mother turned off the lights, and my dad pulled his lighter from his shirt pocket, flicked it to the wicks of the slim white candles in their holders. The heat from the tiny flames rose into a current that set five flat brass angels spinning in a circle that whirred into a carousel of chimes.

As we sat in shadow, I tried to love the elements of our ritual—my father's rare prayer of thanks for the food, his low muttered *amen*, the carols playing on the stereo, the hot chowder in the bowl, the four of us sitting down like a family from a picture book or TV commercial. But reality never met my built-up expectations. The clams in my mouth felt like slippery pockets of snot. "It's the guts and poop," my brother said, and slid out his clammy tongue. The Jell-O salad, which was supposed to taste like sweet oranges, left me gagging on cheese curds that clotted the peach-coloured fluff.

"It's tradition," said my mother when I shuddered at the clams and curds.

"Eat," said my dad. "It's Christmas Eve."

As he leaned back in his chair, the mood in the room shifted. What had been uneasy anticipation—would he come, how long would we wait—drifted into the calm and bright. Though called away from his party, he was jovial, light-hearted, and we were all trying our holiday best, straining for the miraculous as we sat together for our meal.

"Get me some more milk," he said, holding up his glass.

Even his gruff demands couldn't shake loose our little scaffold of peace on earth and goodwill to men. Somewhere in that house, our gifts were hidden, wrapped in shiny paper, ready to be ripped into in a matter of hours, and after we cleared the table and the dishes were washed and dried and put away, we'd watch the TV specials—*Rudolph, Frosty, The Grinch Who Stole Christmas*—and start the countdown to morning, when we'd launch out of bed in the dark and sit in the living room before the stacks of presents piled beneath the lit-up tree, waiting for our dad to finish his morning cigarette and mug of coffee behind the locked bathroom door.

But first, before the momentum toward morning could build any further, my dad set down his empty glass. "We're gonna go for a drive," he said. "To see Grandma Reimer."

She'd been our neighbour, her house a two-minute walk from ours until we moved from Loop Road to the other side of the river, the tracks, the town. On his way home from school, my brother had often knocked on her door and waited on the doorstep while she rustled in her pantry and returned with a cookie or bag of coconut-covered marshmallows, whatever treat she had on hand. Grandma Reimer, long widowed, was someone's grandma, but not ours. She belonged to my dad's side of the family, but indirectly, through a second or third cousin twice-removed. Still, we called her Grandma—*Grossmama*—and we called her two bachelor sons, who lived at the back of her property in a one-room cabin, Uncle Pete and Uncle Jake.

It's not that I dreaded going to Grandma Reimer's house, but it didn't compare to the TV's cartoon elves and top-hatted Frosty laughing up our Christmas Eve. Visiting her felt like duty, the way I would come to feel in adolescence about church, huffing at the ritual of it, wondering what was the point of our Sunday routine, the hymns, the long-winded sermons preached by a monotone, legally blind minister.

"Really?" my mother said to my dad. "We're going?" She sighed, and stacked our dirty supper dishes in the kitchen sink.

"It's tradition," said my dad, wiping his mouth on his sleeve. "You can drive."

GRANDMA REIMER'S HOUSE was dark when we pulled into her driveway.

"She's probably sleeping," said my mother. "Let's come back another day."

But my dad was already out of the passenger seat, tromping up the front steps and knocking. After a moment, the porch light came on, and the door opened a crack. My dad looked back at us still sitting in the idling pickup and waved for us to come.

Grandma Reimer stood in the doorway smiling, smoothing the stray white hairs that had come loose from the braided, coiled bun at the nape of her neck. "Come," she said, drawing us into the dim, tiny house. "Oh, bah, yo," she said, the *yo* her "yes" to our arrival. She led the way into the main room, which functioned as kitchen, dining area, and den. Seated at the table, Uncle Pete and Uncle Jake sat smoking, the air above their heads hazed blue. From its high shelf in the corner of the room, the TV buzzed a fuzzy black-and-white show.

"Hallo," they said, nodding, lifting their cigarette hands.

The uncles sat on a wooden bench with their backs to the wall, dressed alike in dark snap-front work shirts and matching pants with clip-on suspenders. They were a study in contrasts. Uncle Pete was built like a bulldog, jowly and broad-chested. He had a square face and a salt-and-pepper buzz cut. When he smiled, which was often, his eyes narrowed into slits, and his laughter sounded like radio static. Uncle Jake, the younger by several years, wore his thinning hair slicked back into a ducktail. He was lanky and long-faced. Twitchy, he sat with his knee bouncing beneath the table, and to whatever anyone said, he nodded and loudly agreed.

"Merry Christmas," my dad boomed.

"Yeah-yeah-yeah-yeah-yeah," said Uncle Jake, wide-eyed and leaning forward in his seat. Uncle Pete crackled with laughter.

My dad pulled up a chair at the table and started talking in Low German with the uncles. Between puffs on their cigarettes, the three men chewed slices of farmer's sausage set out by Grandma Reimer, who toddled from refrigerator to stove, pantry to kitchen counter, delivering plates of food and cups of coffee and tea to the table. Small and round, shaped like a Russian nesting doll, she wore a home-sewn, elastic-waisted polyester dress in muted florals, thick beige pantyhose, and black lace-up shoes. She was in every way the traditional Mennonite grandmother—bustling, plain, offering food, and more food, and still more food. She spoke almost no English, and what little she knew, she wove together with bits of German. She knew my name, and spoke it to me as she pinched my cheeks and said, "So fat, so fat."

At the table, the men's voices spewed words that sounded like throat-clearing, growly and moist and on the verge of anger, but then they'd tip their heads back and laugh until they started hacking tarry coughs again. Their language, *Plattdeutsch*, was the informal dialect of Mennonites, a cobbled German used for ordinary conversation and barnyard talk, a degradation of the High German reserved for scripture, sermons, and songs. Every few sentences, I caught a fragment of English, or some German word I understood. In *Kaut, Schnee, Mutta, Trock*, I heard cat, snow, mother, truck, but I didn't know enough to fit them together into the conversation happening around the shared ashtray. In the presence of

Uncle Jake and Uncle Pete, my dad loosened, seemed comfortable in his own skin. But for Grandma Reimer, he shifted a little. In her presence, he sloughed his usual bristle for a softness of speech, the way he did around his own mother and in church, on those rare Sundays he still set foot inside it.

While my mother, quiet at the table, sipped her instant coffee and spoke in simple English about the Christmas meal we'd eat tomorrow when the whole Funk family gathered, Grandma Reimer nodded and kept pushing the plates of food toward us. After we'd eaten as much as we could, she rose from the table and, through a door off the kitchen, disappeared into the sound of rustling plastic and clinking glass. She came back carrying two packages.

"Merry Christmas," she said, and held them out to me and my brother.

Our mother had taught us always to say thank you, no matter what the gift might be. What was given you, you took, and took with gratitude, whether or not you liked it. A pair of slippers crocheted from scratchy wool, a make-your-own-potholder kit, a child-sized suitcase with a comb and brush set tucked inside—though not what you might dream of receiving, they still were gifts, and the giver deserved honest thanks.

My brother and I tore into our presents, paper flying to the floor as we unwrapped what Grandma Reimer had chosen from her pantry. For my brother, a small car that raced spring-loaded on fat rubber wheels and whirred an engine noise. For me, a smiling plastic doll, naked in a see-through bag, her wide, unblinking eyes goggling back at me. And for each of us, tucked in with our toys, a cup and saucer in the old

plain style found in the china cabinets of Mennonite grandmothers everywhere, edged in tiny blue flowers.

Our mother cleared her throat and tilted her head toward
us in reminder.

"Thank you," we both said to Grandma Reimer. She smiled,
nodded, and pushed the plate of sausage toward us once again.

"Eat," she said. "Oh, bah, eat."

While my father gossiped gutturally and lit another cigarette, and my mother tried to find the words to bridge the gap
between her and a woman she hardly knew, I sat in my chair,
my cup and saucer tucked aside, and fiddled with my plastic doll. Every time I turned its arm or leg, the limb popped
out of the socket, but the smile on its face never changed. As
Grandma Reimer poured the tea and coffee again and again,
filled and refilled the small white plates with slices of cheese
and bread and meat, and my dad and the uncles talked in a
language beyond me, I watched my brother's toy car zoom
across the linoleum. Over and over, he pulled back the car,
then let it go. The more he reversed its wheels on the floor, the
farther forward it launched, flying ahead with the momentum from its backward drag, the men's voices rising and
falling over the quiet talk of my mother and Grandma Reimer,
the window giving back our faces blurred against the dark,
snow-pocked sky.

AFTER THE UNCLES shook my father's hand, and Grandma
Reimer squeezed my cheeks goodbye, told my brother how
big, how big he'd grown, patted my mother on the forearm,
saying *Merry Christmas*, lilting her voice upward as she

spoke the words, we climbed back into the pickup, yawning and slow. My dad, now clear-eyed and fully awake behind the steering wheel, said how good it was for us to have gone for a visit, that it was important, Grandma Reimer wasn't getting any younger.

"Who knows how long she's got," he said.

Along the road's snow-hush, we drove, the cab of the pickup stuffy and smoky with the heater blowing hot air and the radio carols cranked. The windshield wipers pushed away the snowflakes, clearing our view of what lay ahead. In our wake, a swirl of white and billow of exhaust, evidence of us moving through darkness, rounding the curve, leaving behind the old home on Loop Road and heading toward our new house, Christmas morning only one sleep away.

I held the hollow, bug-eyed doll and knew it wasn't worth naming. It would end up in a bucket of plastic bath toys, and eventually lose all its limbs. On my lap, the cup and saucer clinked with every road bump.

"That's practically antique," my mother said. "You'll want to keep it, put it somewhere safe, so it won't break."

If the cup were full of sweet tea or coffee thick with cream, I'd sit at the table and like a grown-up, hold it to my lips and sip until I hit the sugar at the bottom, then scrape out the syrup, lick every crystal from the spoon. But for now, that cup, empty and old, held nothing for me. Wrapped in tissue paper and stored in a cardboard box, it would be shoved into the basement crawlspace along with baby clothes and toys, old papers and photographs, and books we didn't read anymore but couldn't bear to throw away.

At the bridge, though the road was empty and not a car was in sight, we waited for the light to shift from red to green. That wooden bridge, blackened by years and creosote, would catch fire in a year and burn to a charred skeleton, the flaming trusses splashing and sizzling into the river. A new bridge would rise, wide enough for two lanes to freely pass, but for now, we waited to cross over to the other side. Below us, the ice lay silvery and smooth, hiding the waters darkly moving toward the sea. From deep down, the ground gave up its ancient swell like a cup filled to overflowing, pouring out what it could no longer hold.

By and By, Lord

◇◇◇

IN THE MIDDLE of a dark and quiet afternoon, when all us students in our study carrels pencilled at our work, my head bent over a page of long addition—*carry the one, carry the one*—the silver bell on the desk behind me dinged.

"Children," the teacher said, "look out the window."

For weeks, the ground had been frozen, the dead grass white with frost, but the blank sky, overcast and pale grey, gave nothing—no blue, no thunder, no wind, no sleet. With my classmates, I rushed to the window to witness the shift.

Each year, by the time the season's first snow appeared, I'd lost all memory of last winter's treachery. Gone from my mind—the black-ice highway, the blizzards blowing sideways, the forty-below cold that freezes gasoline. Gone—the bitter wind that burns the skin, numb fingers, numb toes, feet like blocks of wood in boots that won't keep out the chill. Gone, the trudge across the yard to haul more firewood from the shed, my loaded sled tugged up the hill. Gone, my shovel blade scraping across the yard, another fall of snow, another shoveling, and I, another northern kid, caught in winter's loop.

What began as invisible came slowly into view. Pinpricks of silver. Flecks, nearly imperceptible, soloing lazily down. And then cinders drifting from a far-off fire. The sky tearing itself to pieces, letting us have it.

Set free into the courtyard, coatless and still wearing our indoor shoes, my classmates and I ran, scraping the shreds of snow from the dirt and pavement and throwing them into the air so that our hair was dusted white, and our cheeks burned wet and cold. To the sky that fell and failed us, to the God of a season that wounded and stoked our wonder, I tipped my face, I closed my eyes, I opened wide my mouth.

RECESS IN THE school field, we tramped a wide circle in the snow, boots shuffling in the drifts to stamp our track. Inward from the circle, we marked out spokes that ended at a centre hub—the safety zone. Together, we built our game, girls and boys in unity at work, but once the boundary lines were drawn, the hunt began.

One potato, two potato, three potato, four—

We counted fists to choose our predator, the fox to chase the wild geese. Donny—the fast one, the hyperactive one, the boy whose eyes hardened into slits when he smirked—lifted his nose to the cold sky and *yip-yip-yipped* a bark to scatter us, his prey.

With the rest of my classmates, I shot out into the circle and down one of the spokes, taking the ten-second lead to break as far away from danger as I could.

I knew I wasn't fast enough to last, that I needed to steer near the safety zone, but even then, the rule was clear: the geese can pass through, but cannot stay. With every lope, my footsteps dragged a little more, snow-pack on my boot soles and the burden of a heavy coat and ski pants weighing me down, until at my back, the fox was yipping, gaining on me.

In chapel, we learned all about the devil's schemes, his wily tricks and lies, and how he preys on weak and faithless ones. I didn't want it to be me. I didn't want to be the first one taken out, picked off, an easy target. In the open field of white, in the eye-ache glare of sun on snow, I maneuvered my body inside the drawn lines, keeping with the rhythm of the game, slowing when the fox slowed, caught up in the chase and bound by winter.

THE PREACHER'S VOICE, a metronome in monotone, kept time. Long and dragging time. I stretched out on the pew, or tried to, but my mother pushed back to prop me up.

"You're old enough to sit," she whispered in my ear.

I swung my feet. Kicked out my legs and pointed my toes. I picked the pills of lint that dotted my tights.

Sit still, she mouthed, her mother-eyes lit up.

Above me, incandescent light bulbs gridded the ceiling tiles. I tried to count, but lost my place somewhere along row three. Across the aisle, the lady with the facial tic kept trying out a smile, her lips in constant twitch, her glasses rising, falling on her cheeks with every spasm.

"Who shall ascend into the hill of the Lord?" the preacher said, the sermon's scripture passage open in his Bible hand.

I saw it in my mind—the long toboggan hill slicked down by sleds and crazy carpets. Out back behind the school, it crested with laughter, shrieks, and whoops, the promise of the rush.

"Or who shall stand," the preacher intoned, "in His most holy place?"

Before I flew, I had to climb. Every step was a chore, a trudge, a reckoning of sweat and burning lungs. Each time a body rocketed past, a wake of snow spray stung my face and sleeted my eyes. At the top, the ones who waited in line wore smiles. At the bottom, they hollered and high-fived, and punched a fist of victory in the air.

My mother nudged me to pay attention to the preacher's words, but I was lost, gone off wandering in my mind, somewhere in between the psalm and hardback wooden pew, the long ascent through elements that kept the body down.

I WOKE TO Johnny's voice calling his wife's name, calling the whole Cash and Carter family to join him on stage. My mother's winter coat, my makeshift blanket, covered me on the three chairs she'd pulled together for a bed. "Lie down," she'd said, "it's late," and even through the steel-guitar solo and the shuffle of the drums, I slid into sleep, hearing and not hearing as Johnny sang, *I keep a close watch on this heart of mine.*

In the darkened hockey arena, the rink ice covered over with plywood to make a floor, the floods lit Johnny, his right arm crooked high on the body of the guitar. When the song swelled into a musical interlude, he stepped away from the microphone, and as he strummed, pulled back the guitar like a shotgun. My dad, standing to the side with his trucker buddies and card-game pals, tipped his chin up, laughed. "Pretty good," he said, "that man in black."

When June walked back out with her sisters and her daughter, and they stood with Johnny along the front of the stage, the whole audience jumped to their feet, clapping, clapping. Even my mother, who stood guard over me, clapped, rising on her tiptoes to witness the finale.

"Do you want to see?" she said, and pulled me up to stand on the chair beside her. Johnny and June and Rosanne and the rest of the singers and band members were far away, but I could see that June wore a white floor-length dress, and her long hair shone beneath the lights, and she was waving at us. I waved back, believing June Carter Cash could see my blonde head out among the crowd.

Then Johnny started to strum, a steady *chuck-a-chuck-a-chuck-a-chuck*, and June's voice came in sad and lonesome as the night train whistling through our valley. *I was uh standin' by my window on one cold and cloudy day.*

Above us, the rafters hung with flags and pennants won by local hockey teams. Higher still, beyond the ceiling and the roof, the sky was pricked full of holes and falling in shreds, like hints about the home waiting on the other side. On the highway as we'd travelled toward the music, the windshield was a blizzard of flakes. Looked at too long, the snow turned to flying stars, light speed. *Watch out*, my mother said, and gripped the dash, *be careful, Dave*, as my dad hunched over the steering wheel, blinking into the night.

Undertaker, undertaker, please drive slow, sang June Carter Cash as her mother's body rolled away. When the fiddle pulled hard into the song, the whole family crowded around the microphones and in four-part harmony sang, *Will the circle be unbroken, by and by, Lord, by and by*. I pulled my mother's heavy coat around me, slipped my arms into the puffy, too-long sleeves, and felt the collar's cool fabric on my neck. I leaned against her back, close enough to smell her hair—the wind and earth and snow-damp warmth of it, and to see the double cowlick of her crown, two whorls of soft brown joined but curling away from each other. *By and by, Lord*, we all sang together, *by and by*.

AS WE WALKED the line that moved around the edges of the sanctuary, I held my mother's hand. The whole room murmured with hushed voices, the shush of shoes and winter boots shuffling over carpet. At the front, the organ and the piano played quiet hymns, and a small table waited with a vase of white flowers beside a long wooden box. The top half of the box lay open, the lid cocked back on its hinges, like a magician's trick with the lady sawed in two.

"Don't look," my mother said, and pulled me close against the scratchy wool of her coat, but I only hid one eye and left the other open so I could look out toward the casket as we inched by. In the folds of the white shiny fabric lay a black suit, a man with his arms tucked straight at his sides, his white shirt collar buttoned at the throat. His face lay slack, eyelids smooth and bluish, cheeks gaunt, and skin dull grey, the ash of last year's fire pit scattered on the ice for tread.

My mother's voice, panicked and soprano the night we skidded down the highway past the Pine Country Inn, came back to me. The road too slick to steer, and our green Oldsmobile sliding past the turn-off as she gripped the wheel, pumped the brakes, said, *I can't stop, I can't stop.* She breathed a high and drawn-out vowel that made me think we'd end up in another town or in the ditch. Past the truck weigh scales, the veterinary clinic, and the lumber mill's incinerator glowing smoke in the night sky, we barrelled into the snowflake-streaked darkness. I was sure that we were headed to our death, that soon, the flashing sirens would be called to us in our crumpled heap of metal.

All through the service, I watched the open coffin, Great-Grandpa's pointed nose and cheekbone visible in profile from where we sat. I wondered if what my mother said was true—that once, a woman had sat up in the middle of her own funeral and asked for a drink of water. But nowadays, said my mother, the lips of the dead are sewn shut.

While the preacher spoke in German in the quiet sanctuary, I listened for the rustle of the casket's satin lining, for the sound of an old man's voice straining through stitches. As we bowed our heads in prayer, I peeked through squinted eyes to see if that body might arch up like Lazarus from his tomb when Jesus said, "Come forth." When the preacher shut the lid, and my dad and his brothers stood on either side of the coffin and carried it down the aisle toward the long black car that waited outside the front doors of the church, I hoped Great-Grandpa was dead, fully and completely dead, never to wake in his frozen plot beneath the drifts of snow, never to knock his knuckles on the ceiling of his wooden box and holler to be let out. I wanted him to lie forever in the dirt, mouldering until that final day when the trumpet call of Heaven cracked the earth wide open and all our bodies rose up from our graves clean and new, our bones dressed and ready for the angels to usher us into the cloud.

I THOUGHT I'D killed him.

In the middle of the driveway, on our Honda Big Red three-wheeler, I cranked the handlebars as far left as they'd go and revved the throttle to turn a tight circle on the hard-packed snow. With every revolution, we gathered momentum, me on the machine and my brother on the inflated inner tube tied behind with a thirty-foot length of rope. Belly-down, he bounced each time the tube caught a ridge or dip, but held on tightly. With every donut spun, we edged toward the bank of snow my dad had ploughed along the yard. At the end of the taut rope, my brother slid in wide orbit until at last, he hit the bank, his body jetted airborne with limbs outstretched— stunt man, fall guy, six-million-dollar boy—bionic as he flew in momentary hover.

The empty tube slid toward me on its slackened rope. When I turned Big Red around and cut the engine, the open field of snow along the driveway lay blank and brotherless.

I thought I'd killed my brother, disappeared him, erased him into air. All the kid-sister terrors I doled out—my lippy quipping, my victim cheek, the way I'd lure his temper with a well-aimed sneer, then tattle when he raged—flew back to me. *Dear God, dear God, dear God*, I prayed, not knowing how to ask for resurrection.

When, up through the crust, his gloved fist punched, and his bright-red helmet crashed through the white, I felt the cold air sting my eyes to tears. My brother, spitting out and shaking off the snow, stamping through the waist-high drift, had come back to me whole.

"Let's go." he said. "Again."

TO MAKE THE perfect angel, you have to leap into a clean, untrampled patch of snow. You have to plant yourself, then fall straight back. As the ground receives you, let your body go, and trust that it won't break. Your spine won't snap. The breath that leaves your lungs will soon return. After the soft *whump*, lie still a moment. This is what it feels like to sleep inside the cold. Cocooned. Snug in the snow-hush.

Above you, stars like stitches in a quilt adorn the dusk. Find the Little Bear's North Star, the compass mark to point you home, if ever you get lost. Find Big Dipper tipping out a scoop of bruised and blue-black sky. You haven't learned the names of all the other constellations, only know that God created them, spoke darkness into light, and from that light made stars, and called them each by name. *Dolores. Corinne. Bryan. Frederick.* You wonder if the stars know who they are, have any clue who hung them with the moon.

Swooped up and down in flutter form, your arms make wings. Your legs, kicked out and in, swish the shape of an angel's robe. Like every night, the signal comes. The porch light by the front door flickers on, casting glitter on the whiteness of the yard. No halo marks your head, but when you climb up from the ground, the snow around you glows.

AT THE FIRST signs of freedom, when the icicles that hung along the eaves began to drip and the crust of snow over the yard trickled to slush, my brother and I pulled our bicycles from the shed. We pedalled up and down the driveway, skidding in the mud and ice slicks, riding out the new release. Like Aslan the lion soaring over Narnia and turning the white kingdom back to green and flowers and leaves on trees, thaw began to wake the scrubby birches and poplars into bud, velveting the willows, sugaring the wind against my cheeks. With the rush of water unlocked, with the trill from the high branches and telephone wires, with the wet world's canticle in praise of spring, I joined, my whole self singing as I flew behind my brother, wheeling away from winter, however temporal my flight.

SPRING

The Higher
Kingdom

◇◇◇

EVERYTHING HELD THE possibility of God. Sun through
the kitchen window stretched like the first waterlogged
rainbow above the ark. Last summer's bloodstains on
the chopping block echoed the Passover's painted doorframe.
Even my sparkle-spackled bedroom ceiling glinted a melody in my head as I lay awake, humming a song about Jesus
coming back *in the twinkling of an eye*. The world and all its
elements reverberated like Sunday-school lessons pointing
toward a higher kingdom. Nothing was exempt from meaning,
from meaning more than itself, from speaking beyond the sky
in symbol and sign. Nowhere was off-limits for a voice to hint
through clouds: *Look, I'm here, I'm everywhere*, which was
why, on a springtime Saturday morning, at the centre of town,

I stood beside my brother in a crowd of people, watching the sky, buoyant with hope.

A week prior, the headline of our local newspaper had advertised the "First Annual Ping-Pong Ball Drop," an event sponsored by the village municipality to promote local businesses and community spirit. The article promised coupons, cash savings, and prizes galore—and the excitement of watching a helicopter dump thousands of ping-pong balls into the Co-op parking lot. "All ages welcome!" it said. "Everyone a winner!"

We'd come for the thrum and thrill of something new, for the surprise of the unknown. Around me gathered truckers in lumberjack flannel, cowboys in their boots and jean jackets, teenagers with shaggy hair hanging in their eyes, moms in jogging suits, moms in slacks and sweater sets, and kids, my closest rivals. Everyone buzzed with the same anticipation. Even the Pennsylvania Dutch, those other, stricter Mennonites who kept to themselves and did not mix much with the rest of us, had come in force. *Pinheads*, my dad called them, for the way the women looked in their white bonnet-like head coverings—like plastic-beaded straight pins—and for what he deemed their ignorance at not allowing chrome on the vehicles they drove because they believed the silver flashiness too worldly. They waited at the edge of the assembly, the serious men and boys in their dark clothes standing apart from the females in their simple dresses. All the girls my age wore their hair pulled back in long, tight braids, and I wondered if that might give them an edge. My throat tightened with my heart's adrenaline thud. I brushed my bangs back from my face. The competition was making me jittery.

Before anything had appeared in the sky, I heard it— the far-off *thwack-thwack-thwack* like a wooden paddle slapping water at high speed, or a machine gun firing down a threat. Then—there, there—I saw it, too—the helicopter rising from behind a tree-topped hill and banking into the valley. An awe-filled gasp dominoed through the crowd. A man's deep baritone called out, "Get ready! Here she comes!"

Like everyone around me, I started shuffling forward, toward what I wasn't sure yet, but the will of the crowd overtook and I followed. My brother, slipping ahead, had the gleam of pursuit in his eyes, like when he set off into the trees with his slingshot. The helicopter banked a sharp right, and suddenly I was turning, too, caught up in the flock of bodies, jogging, then stopping, then starting again. From an aerial vantage, our horde of hundreds must have looked like a shape-shifting amoeba, struggling toward the promise of the prize, wobbling and warping as we tried to anticipate the chopper's path.

It was the first time I'd felt the energy of a mob, at least outside of a church service. I was accustomed to standing in my pew and with my fellow congregants belting out verses one, three, and four of "All Hail the Power." I was used to being part of the sacred throng, but outside in the early-May coolness, we were uncontained, loosened from any structure, and tilting toward chaos.

A mustached man in a ballcap began waving his arms over his head, as if in a bid to lure the chopper closer. "Hey!" he yelled. "Over here!" Like a contagion, his waving and yelling caught hold, and soon everyone was doing it—our noise a mix of shrieks, hoots, and bellows. I raised my hands above my head, supplicating to the far-off forestry service helicopter like a stranded desert-island child catching a first glimpse of rescue. I'd lost sight of my brother's bright-blue windbreaker, but I was sure he was waving his hands, too. How could he not be? Everyone else was doing it. Somewhere at the edge of the parking lot, my mother clutched her purse, waiting for the mayhem to subside.

As the helicopter veered down, its side door opened. The shape of a man appeared—dark hair, flash of a red jacket. A huge black bag. And the man's hands working to open it. Like Christmas morning before the gifts, like a bonfire before gasoline and the lit match, like the darkened hush before the choir's first note, my exhilaration surged. The helicopter circled again and held its hover. Out of the heavy-duty garbage bag spilled a cluster of white dots. What looked like a thick cloud of hailstones began to break loose, scattershot in the sky, falling and falling toward my outstretched hands, my thumping heart. Suddenly, nothing about our small town felt small. The usual quiet of our slow roads and sidewalks crescendoed to the raucous noise of rotor chop and crowd chatter. The world was as wide as the blue open sky, broken only by the noise of a whirring machine pouring out its bounty.

If ever there was a time to ask for God's favour, this was it. In my head, I thought a prayer that went something like, *Please, God, pick me, make me win*—the kind of words my dad said every Wednesday night as the lottery balls popcorned in their metal cage, and one by one, their numbers were revealed live on television by a news anchor and his glossy, lipsticked assistant. *One day*, my dad said, *one day, it'll be my turn.*

Above the parking lot, the ping-pong balls drifted down. Wind currents caught them, shifted their course. It grew clear that anyone who wanted to snatch the balls in mid-air would need some serious agility or a fluke miracle. Around me, men and women zigzagged. Some lost their footing, skidded, wiped out belly-down on the ground, but jumped up again and kept following the wind's path.

As the first wave of balls began to land, a whole new level of intensity gripped the crowd. Punctuating the plastic clatter on the asphalt were the cries and groans of full-grown men as they scrambled, dove, shot their bodies to the ground, as if pitching themselves into water. Around me, balls bounced like jumping beans, rolled beneath vehicles. As I grabbed for them, other hands grabbed, too. A bent-over kerchiefed grandma sideswiped me as I reached. Like a scavenger, a boy swooped by and scooped up two nearby balls. Women crawled on scraped and bleeding knees, their brows furrowed and jaws clenched. An old man who minutes earlier had tapped his cigarette ash into a puddle and smiled at me now seemed ready to clamp his false teeth onto anyone who crossed his path. When a secondary spill of balls fell on top of Aunt Lavonne's station wagon, two guys climbed over the hood and roof without hesitation, scuffing the powder-blue paint with their boots and snapping off the antenna as they scrambled for the prize.

For all my grabbing, I came up empty-handed. Those who had balls in hand clutched them close, tight-fisted, but when I stood up and looked around the parking lot, balls were still rolling loose and free over the asphalt. No one seemed to care.

Next to me, a lady gripped a ping-pong ball with a number inked in black. Finally, I understood the game. Only some were winning balls. The blank ones counted for nothing.

Above the brief lull in the skittering and jostling, the helicopter hovered still, louder and lower than ever, and about to dump its final bag. This time, savvy to the wind, I moved to the edge of the crowd, hoping that fewer bodies surrounding me might mean a greater chance at the balls bouncing to the outskirts. When the last load let loose, balls confettied the parking lot. I scouted for the ones marked with black ink, tossing away the blanks as I scrambled toward them. I was singular in purpose, focused on the goal, and scooped up a number 23. Those around me faded to the nameless and faceless. Somewhere in the pandemonium, my brother ran after his own prize, but I'd stopped watching for his blue windbreaker. When a lady and I reached for the same winning ball, I didn't back down, and jerked it away and stuffed it in my coat pocket before she had a chance to see the number written on it.

From the helicopter's high, omniscient vantage, I was a blip amid other blips scrounging on the ground, one yellow speck in a speckled network, but still, I felt strangely spotlighted. Like God's eye was fixed on me with favour. Like my striving to win translated into glory, and the degree of my desire intensified into a prayer that refused to go unanswered. After the helicopter's door slid shut and it broke its hover over us, after it disappeared behind the hill and into clouds, the crowd headed toward the Co-op. Inside, at the back of the store, volunteers in red Co-op T-shirts sat at a row of tables, doling out prizes corresponding to the numbered ping-pong balls.

As I stood in line beside my brother, a girl my age walked past carrying a jumbo jar of Magic Bubbles. Another girl held the string of a helium-filled balloon emblazoned with a smiley face and the Co-op logo. Prizes shuffled by. A giant plush bear with a bow around its neck. A sand pail and shovel set. A toolkit. A bunch of bananas. Some folks held slips of paper, coupons for discounts on goods and services. Buy one tank of gas, get a free Shell air freshener. Ten per cent off a watermelon at Shoppers Food Mart.

When I reached the front of the line, my two numbered ping-pong balls were slick with clammy palm sweat. I handed them over to a red-shirted lady, who ran her finger down a sheet of paper printed with columns.

"Number 23," said the lady. "And number 52." She looked up at me and smiled. "Back in a minute, sweetie." She disappeared behind flaps of black rubber into what looked like a warehouse buzzing with action and bodies and stacks of boxes.

My knees burned when I tensed them, the skin tender from crawling on asphalt and now chafing against the corduroy fabric. I expected something good, if not grand. A sparkle-seated bicycle with streamers sprouting from the handles. An inflatable swimming pool or Hot Wheels racetrack or even a grocery sack full of candy. I believed I'd earned it, was worthy of it. *The eyes of the Lord are in every place*, taught the proverb, *beholding the evil and the good*. Surely, I'd been good enough for God to will the winning balls toward my outstretched hands.

The red-shirted Co-op lady returned carrying a smallish cardboard box. Behind her, a red-shirted man hefted a huge, lumpy burlap bag. "You've won," she said, "a portable camp stove!" She paused while the man set down the sack with an *oomph*. "And fifty pounds of potatoes!"

That life would disappoint, that I wouldn't always get what I wanted—these things I'd caught wind of in the way caskets opened at the front of the church, in mosquito bites and wasp stings, in liver and onions for supper instead of burgers and fries, but that something about me didn't deserve the best— this was a new thought glimmering in me. Out there in the crowd, another girl had caught God's shining eye. Maybe she was tiny as a sprite, a pretty thing who never stuck her tongue out at kids on passing school buses, who didn't whisper into a classmate's ear that Tammie smelled like pee and dirty underwear. This girl was surely the one Christ pulled close when he said, "Suffer the little children to come unto me." While Jesus laid his gentle hand on her head, I stood on the sidelines, waiting for him to notice me.

Flush-cheeked and tight-throated, I walked past those still standing in line to claim their prizes. Beside me, my mother carried the box with the camp stove in it. She tried to sound enthusiastic. "This will be great for when the power goes out," she said. Behind us, the red-shirted man trailed with the potatoes, cradling the sack over his shoulder like a body off the battlefield as he followed us to our car.

"Fifty pounds is a heck of a lot of potatoes," he said as he heaved them into the trunk.

Though my mother never said it, the last thing we needed was more potatoes. We had a root cellar full of last summer's harvest. We ate potatoes almost every night for supper.

Mashed, hash-browned, boiled, baked, scalloped, in soups and stews, sliced and fried. The humble potato, my mother would say, the true peasant's food.

BACK HOME, I wandered over to the shop, where my father and a few trucker buddies sat around the woodstove with their drinks and the radio crooning the local country-music station.

"Win anything?" my dad asked.

All the men laughed when they heard about the potatoes, that burlap sack now leaning up against the carport's stucco like a good joke.

"What're you gonna do with fifty pounds of potatoes?" said Sparky. Heavy-lidded, he slumped on his block of wood with his can of beer. I shrugged. "If you want to sell 'em," he said, "I'm buyin'."

My mother helped me load the potatoes into the red wagon, and I pulled it across the yard and into the shop. Sparky hoisted the sack into the back of his pickup and pulled his wallet from his pants pocket.

"Go buy yourself something fun, Blondie," he said, and handed me a ten-dollar bill. "But maybe not potatoes." His laughter crackled.

As I walked back toward the house, the money clutched in my fist didn't feel quite like a winning ticket. More like a backup plan, or a consolation prize. If water could be turned to wine, and that was called a miracle, then fifty pounds of russets swapped for cash might be okay. I had ten dollars to spend on anything I wanted—a cap gun, dinky cars, fishing tackle, jacks—and I had a camp stove to set up in the tree fort so I could imagine myself into an orphan learning to fend for herself in the wild. With scoured old pots and pans from the basement crawlspace, I'd cook pinecones and sand and clay, and chop up thistles and dandelion heads into a cold, murky stew, the food of a starving child hankering for scraps, eager for anything to eat. Even without the charcoal lit to embers, it wouldn't be hard to pretend a fire. I'd make do with what I got, and learn that when you're thirsty enough, even water scooped from a puddle in the ditch tastes sweet. Even the sky, unzipping its blue, could pour forth the abundance of the earth, if I was willing to receive, hold open my hands and catch whatever light might fall.

Ask Now
the Beasts

◇◇◇

But ask now the beasts,
and they shall teach thee...
—JOB 12:7

NO OTHER BIRD sings *chick-a-dee-dee-dee*, my mother
said, the way the chickadee can.

Except for the piano keys I plunked, I had no signature song. In the choir, I was one kid among a row of boys and
girls, and we all sang someone else's tune, a score composed
for children's voices, simple and unadorned. When I looked
out the window at the chickadees flitting on the feeder, I studied them for some trait of a maker blinking through. As they
jittered and scratched at the suet and sunflower seeds, the
shells flew to the dirt, their black-capped heads moving like

figures in a stop-motion animation. I wanted to read those birds and know what God was thinking when he invented their buffy feathers, black bibs, round heads, when he hollowed their bones for flight. God had a master plan, but what and why, I still hadn't figured out. I wanted to know the truth behind the mystery, to be able to decipher the code etched into the universe. I wanted to listen like a prophet, to hear what only the wise ones hear, so that I, too, could have my own chapter in a thick, leather-bound book, like Joseph and Gideon and Esther, all those famous lives of faith. I wanted my life to be worthy of a Bible story, illuminated in full colour.

"All of nature speaks of its maker," said our school principal, Mr. Schroeder, which is why, he explained, we study both books written by the Creator—the Holy Bible, and the book of the natural world, with all the chapters in its glorious design.

Like I'd learned in our school's weekly devotional time, I leaned on the pigpen fence and studied our quintet of pigs to see what God might be saying. As they wallowed in late-spring mud, their snouts, rooting in the sludge of their own poop, came up brown and glistening. Their small eyes wheedled, and when I dumped a bucket of slop into the trough, they squealed and snapped at each other like wild boars, the kind that would gore an old yeller dog. Only weeks ago, I'd fed them by hand, and before that, when they'd first arrived, swaddled each of them in turn in a flannel doll blanket. On the fresh straw in the corner of the shed, I'd cradled a piglet, scratched its wiry pink chin until it fell asleep in my arms. But now, in their filth and gluttony, they'd gone primal, forgetting my kindness.

Even my closest animal companion, Leslie, the patched tabby I'd found as a kitten in a hollow log, seemed to have forsaken me. The one who used to follow me like a stealthy shadow had grown aloof ever since Packsack, the trap- per who lived part of the year in a trailer in our yard, had stuffed the cat headfirst into a length of stovepipe. After the jackknife-quick castration, Leslie shot into the bushes, leaving droplets of blood in a trail on the dirt. My dad shook Packsack's hand and paid him his case of beer. A couple days later, the cat slunk out of the woods, healed up but wary of human hands, including mine.

I watched our black dog, too, for signs that God was speaking, but mostly, she just licked herself, barked whenever someone drove into the yard, and scooched her bum along the grass. In the crowns of poplar trees, the crows flocked, their scrawk and screech like fingernails on a chalkboard. God's voice said nothing to me. Squirrels sketched the yard in zigzags, scouting and scratching for clues to last autumn's cache of nuts and seeds, but I remained clueless to what the maker of all squirrels might be trying to say.

EVERY WEDNESDAY AFTERNOON, our primary grades tromped single-file out of the classroom, down the stairs and hallway, and into the small chapel where we held morning worship. We plopped down on the weary dun-coloured carpet, elbowing for space closest to the chair on the podium, anything to be near Mr. Schroeder and his big brown book. When he walked through the door at the back of the sanctuary, we settled into our best behaviour, we girls quiet and

prim, the boys quitting their bloody knuckle fights. Even
the rowdies, the ones held almost daily for lunchtime deten-
tion, sat up straighter for Mr. Schroeder. When, at the end of
a chapel sermon, he asked all the students to repeat after him,
"Good, better, best, let's never rest, until our good is better and
our better is the best!" I chanted loudly and with conviction,
certain I was speaking a passage of scripture that would trans-
form me with ever-increasing glory into the likeness of a saint.

In his suit and tie, with his glossy hair trimmed to school-
regulation standards—off the collar and above the ear—Mr.
Schroeder was the closest representation of holiness I knew.
To sit at his feet in that cold little chapel was what I imagined
being near to God must feel like—scary, awesome, and smelling of Old Spice. I couldn't help but inch closer to him as he
spoke, yet fearing I'd say or do something wrong, commit
some sin that might banish me from his presence.

Mr. Schroeder held the big brown devotional book the
same way he held the Bible—with a grip that said: *This book
is important.* The leather-bound volume was one in a series
of books about the animal kingdom and was our text for
Wednesday Devotions, the school's weekly time set apart to
study spiritual truth, to learn about God and the wide realm
of his creation. Every chapter in the big brown book was ded-
icated to a different creature that crawled, crept, slithered,
swam, stalked, or flew. Migration maps, feeding habits, aver-
age wingspan, habitat—all these facts and figures showed us
more about the natural world.

I loved that brown book, the heft and fatness of it, the
cover's depiction of a grizzly bear standing on its back legs,

paws raised, snout scenting the air. Each week, Mr. Schroeder opened to a new chapter, and as he read aloud, his words made a creature step from the savannah, flap up from the thicket, or leap from the dark waters. Every creature, by its natural, God-ordained instincts and behaviours, displayed its Maker's traits, and preached to us, those highest in the chain of creatures, how best to live. The great horned owl, hunting nocturnally to feed its young, demonstrated loyalty and sacrifice. The wolverine, rejecting all distractions, fought off its predators. The Eastern hognose snake, when faced with overwhelming odds, responded with creative resourcefulness.

After the character sketch of the highlighted creature, Mr. Schroeder turned the page and read a companion story, in which we learned about a person from the Bible, a man or woman whose life was meant to echo the traits of whatever creature had come before. After the American coot, we learned about Esther, a beautiful young orphan who turned from a secret Jew into a queen and proved that just like the coot, it's important to unite with those of like mind to conquer evil. After the bobcat, the four lepers appeared, knowing and being where God intended them to be, all so that they could receive a blessing. After the kangaroo rat, Dorcas, full of good words and acts of charity. After the sand wasp, Gideon, who went from a coward hiding in a winepress to a mighty warrior leading his people to victory in battle. From "Abigail and the Whistling Swan" to "Young King Hezekiah and the Black-Headed Gull," animal and human united to teach us about life as God intended, the beasts and Bible characters espousing the same truth, displaying the glory of creation.

From "The Beaver," we learned the importance of order-liness, of good grooming and cleanliness. The beaver, the big brown book told us, is a skilled and industrious rodent that builds its home from sticks and mud. Every lodge has two rooms, the first for drying off—like the cloakroom where we hung our coats and lined up our boots—and the second for family living, like where the TV set blared cartoons after school.

"The beaver, *castor canadensis*," read Mr. Schroeder, "works energetically from sunrise to sundown."

We learned that the beaver uses its flat, broad tail to steer like a rudder as it swims and to slap a danger warning on the water. Because beavers spend so much time being wet, their fur has two layers—the inner, short layer to keep them warm, and the longer outer hairs to create a waterproof suit. Every day, the beaver grooms itself and others in its colony, using the oil from castor glands on its own belly to coat its fur and keep the water out. Mr. Schroeder held the book open and high so we could see the illustrations of the dam, the lodge, and the neatly groomed, sleek-coated rodent with its four incisors glinting.

"Because it keeps itself so clean, the beaver remains free of parasites, which plague creatures less concerned with good grooming," he said, then licked his thumb and lifted the page. "And now we'll hear the story of the penitent woman."

"What's 'penitent'?" said Wesley Peacock, round-headed, big-toothed, peering through thick glasses. He was the boy whose nose never stopped running, the one who hyperventi-lated when he cried, which was often, and easily, and almost always during P.E. class.

"We'll come to that soon," said Mr. Schroeder, his voice slow and smooth. He held up the book and began to read again, this time a true story about a woman who lived in the time of Jesus.

In Mr. Schroeder's book, the animal and the human narratives remained separate, belonging to their own domains, but in my mind's eye, they always appeared side by side, the line between them blurring when he turned the page. This time, the beaver and a woman in Biblical clothes—robe, sandals, a covering for her head—flashed into shared terrain, the house of Simon the Pharisee, where Jesus had been invited for supper. Because women weren't invited to eat with men, and because this woman was sinful, "very sinful," said Mr. Schroeder, the Pharisees didn't want her there.

"But why was she so sinful?" Wesley asked, sniffing his glasses back up the bridge of his nose. "What were her sins?"

"Well." Mr. Schroeder paused. "Let's just say that she had not behaved like a godly woman."

A *godly woman*, I knew, didn't smoke or cuss, didn't wear bright lipstick or mini-skirts. I thought of the wives of my father's trucker buddies, of their rouged cheeks and blue eyeshadow and smoky laughter when someone cracked a dirty joke at the card table. A godly woman wore dresses with the hem below her knees and kept her hair long, brushed one hundred strokes every night before bed to make it shine. Like Miss Hornsby, our music teacher, a godly woman closed her eyes and swayed when she sang in church, and wore a prayer cap on her head, and owned a Bible that, when opened, showed loose pages and verses underlined in red and blue ink.

When the sinful woman entered the house where Jesus was eating supper with the Pharisees, she knelt at his feet and began to cry. I could picture her there, sobbing into his sandals, her tears wetting his toes. And I could see the beaver, too, hunched beside her, the slow thumping of its tail on the floor like a *there, there* consolation.

"The sinful woman, crying and kneeling at Jesus's feet," said Mr. Schroeder, "broke open an alabaster jar, and—"

"What's alabaster?"

We glared at Wesley. Someone hissed *shut up*. Mr. Schroeder took a deep breath and surveyed us with eyes that said, *I'm tired of it, too, but let's all be like Jesus.*

The sinful woman broke open her expensive jar and poured out myrrh, the same gift brought by the wise men who came from the East when Jesus was born, a perfume that people rubbed on the bodies of the dead to hide the smell of rot. She anointed Jesus's feet with that myrrh. Her tears mixed with the fragrance, and she used her long, black hair to wipe his feet. At least, I imagined it as long and black, shining when the light caught it.

"And in doing so," said Mr. Schroeder, "the sinful woman became the penitent woman."

Wesley shot his fat hand in the air. I fought the urge to slap it down.

"And *penitent*," said Mr. Schroeder. Wesley's hand wilted back to his lap. "*Penitent* means she was sorry for the things that she'd done wrong, all the many mistakes she'd made."

As far as east is from the west, said the Bible—that's how far her sins were removed from her, explained Mr. Schroeder.

What was she at the beginning, she was no longer. A true transformation. She became a new woman, a new creation. He thunked shut the big brown book and said, let's bow our heads in prayer, and ask God to make us like the penitent woman, and the beaver, too, who both practiced cleanliness and good grooming, purity of the body and of the heart.

I couldn't help but see the beaver and that woman leaving the Pharisees' feast together, moving down a narrow, dusty road, a fur shadow ambling beside a willowy silhouette. Maybe to the Sea of Galilee they walked, side by side, silent, and at the shoreline sat to dip their toes in the water, look out across the waves, the woman holding her broken, empty perfume jar in her lap, the beaver raking its sharp claws over its belly, even through the woman's long hair that smelled like a forest, like the resin of a split tree, balmy and dark.

As Mr. Schroeder led us in a prayer that we might learn from the ways of the beaver, that we would be just like that woman pouring out her best perfume on Jesus, that all our sins to be washed away, I peered through squinted eyes at my classmates. Bowed heads and matching uniforms sat cross-legged on the rug. I was one creature in a small flock gathered at the feet of our present shepherd, learning how to hear a higher voice inside the clutter and noise. Inside the fidgety shuffling and scratching and breathing of the bodies around me, I closed my eyes and listened for it—for the rare, exalted song that inscribed the universe with clues, for the sound of the one who'd shadow me, who'd lead me to still waters, and once there, teach me the song my own voice made.

The Typewriter

◇◇◇

I **N THE BASEMENT** room where my mother kept her adding
machine and bookkeeping ledgers, I sat at the desk in a
steno chair and waited for my first instruction, for the dis-
embodied voice to tell me what to do.

Fingers in position on the home keys, the voice said.
Ready? Now let's begin.

Inside the crackle of the record's vinyl, the man's words,
smooth and baritone as a radio host, commanded.

a-s-d-f space
;-l-k-j space

Over and over, I repeated the ordered keys, following
along with Lesson One of the Smith-Corona Touch Typing
Course.

a-s-d-f space
;-l-k-j space

Return carriage.

Each key-strike on the blank sheet of paper made my letters appear official and important, superior to the printing
and cursive that filled my notebooks. The typewriter had
been a gift from my parents, my mother imagining for me
a future career in office administration, thinking I might
like to learn how to type, to pretend the role of a secretary
who filled out forms and answered the ever-ringing telephone. But as I punched down the keys, as the machine's
thin metal bars hammered the ribbon and inked the page,
and as the carriage dinged for its next return, I felt my spine
straighten, my body shift into someone smarter, someone
who might do more than sit primly at a receptionist's desk.
Someone who might write a book, the kind real people would
actually read.

Ours was not a bookish family, but we liked books. At least,
my mother, my brother, and I did. Each week, we lugged full
bags of borrowed books to the returns counter at our town's
small library, then checked out new stacks, my brother heading for the Westerns and me to the racks of glossy juvenile
paperbacks. My mother's bedside table displayed her ded-
icated reading habits, with its Bible, *Daily Bread* monthly
devotional, gardening texts, and whatever historical novel she
was working through. Across the bed, my dad's nightstand
lay comparatively bare, with his glass of water, bunched-up

handkerchief, nasal spray, and a radio that played country music on low volume all through the night.

Other than the Ritchie Brothers auction catalogue, with its shiny full-colour pages advertising heavy machinery, the only thing I ever saw my father read was the local newspaper, and even then, he rarely glanced beyond the headlines. At nights, when my brother and I sat listening as our mother read aloud from *The Chronicles of Narnia*, my dad snoozed on the living room carpet, the TV on low, head and shoulders propped on a giant cushion, hands tucked beneath his cheek like a child posed in sleep. Never once did he read us a story, and never once did I ask why. I wondered sometimes if he even knew how to read. He'd left school at the eighth grade, a fact he often repeated when he saw me doing homework at the kitchen table, but he'd left by choice, I thought, hadn't been forced to quit by his father, sent out into the world of work to bring home extra wages for the family, his own story bending to another's will.

At the typewriter, trying to keep my head up, my eyes on the copy, and my wrists relaxed, I pressed on, fingers over the keys, following the man's voice.

a-s-d-f space
;-l-k-j space

Return carriage.
Stop typing.

THE WORDS, AND the urge to stitch them together, had begun with another gift.

"It's a diary," Aunt Pauline had called, over the Christmas noise. "A place to write what happens in a day. Somewhere to keep your secrets."

I'd sat on the living room linoleum at Grandpa and Grandma Funk's, amid the chaos of crumpled wrapping paper, fussing babies, smoking uncles, and battery-operated toys, and slipped the tiny gold key into the lock that clasped the red book shut. With a turn and click, the diary unlocked and released a slim white pen. I opened to the beginning, January 1, 1981, and on the blue-ruled page, wrote:

> *Today is Christmas.*
> *I am writing in my new diary.*
> *Shhhh.*

At school, my pencil traced someone else's letters, following the dotted lines so that the letters took their proper shapes and turned into words, and the words turned into sentences. In the blank spaces in my workbooks, I wrote answers to questions about someone else's story.

> What is the name of Ace's lamb?
> *Baa-Baa*
> What colour is the lamb's wool?
> *White*
> Where is the lamb hiding?
> *Behind the tree*

But alone in my bedroom, behind a locked door, I wrote with my skinny pen in my red pocket diary:

146

There are some things
in my heart that I need
To get rid of that I need
To get rid of them I—
really get rid of them
really really really really
I need to get rid of—
them

> *Jesus said*
> *you are a little—*
> *scared but*
> *don't be scared*

Every lie, every black thought and harsh word, every *pig, jerk, stupid-face, idiot, loser, bugger-off, moron*—they sang on the page. I felt it—the angel who kept records in the Book of Life, standing at my back, leaning over me with a giant quill, and bearing witness as I signed my name. Words, I knew, held power—*the power of life and death*, said the preacher as he read from the Bible. *In the beginning was the Word and the Word was with God, and the Word was God*—it was a verse I'd heard over and over, even memorized for Sunday-school class to earn a pencilled check mark beside my name. I loved the rhythm of it, the way that verse pumped like pedals on a bicycle, its syllables pulsing *Word* and *God*. Spoken aloud, it sounded like a magic spell, an incantation strong enough to bend the listener toward its truth and make them a believer.

MR. JORDAN, THE school bus driver, sat behind the wheel
morning and afternoon, steering us over icy roads, through slush and rain and the heat of Indian summer. When the busload grew raucous, he shouted into his rearview mirror, "Quiet down!" Though his bushy salt-and-pepper beard never betrayed proof, I was sure he wore a constant frown. We kids held a common theory—that Mr. Jordan was a mean and angry man who hated children, all children, and only drove the bus so he could yell at us. His rules were a long list of no's, which he enforced with the rigour of a cop. *No eating, no drinking. No foul language. No fighting. No standing when the bus is moving.* Shelly Reinhardt swore she once saw Mr. Jordan grab a kindergartener by the hood and fling him back into his seat when he stood up before the bus came to a complete stop.

"He's not a mean man," said my mother, when I complained about Mr. Jordan. "He writes poetry, you know."

All I knew of poetry came from the Little Golden Book version of *A Child's Garden of Verses.* Robert Louis Stevenson's poems, with their accompanying illustrations, left me feeling like I was alone in a summer bedroom, with the curtains breeze-lifted and the naptime air cool and dim and quiet. I read the verses again and again, letting their music strike a cadence in me. Images of the sea, of boats, rain, a cow, and the child's shadow, though familiar, were made strange in the poem's unspooling sentences. When the shadow lay in bed like a lazybones and refused to join the child in the noonday sun, I understood the riddle of the image but still felt eerie when I closed the book, as if a mirror had been held up to my own face, as if, in how the words were stitched together, I'd been told a secret about myself.

148

I don't know how the idea came, or what gave me the courage to act on it, but one morning, when I climbed the steps into the bus and Mr. Jordan said "Good morning" in a voice that was half gruff, half kindness, I said, "Will you write me a poem?"

"A poem?" he said. He leaned back in his seat, adjusted his cap. He wore the same thick, black-framed glasses as my dad. "You want a poem?"

I nodded, queasy at the thought that he might yell or tell me to sit down, be quiet, stay put.

"I'll see what I can do," he said, and cranked shut the folding doors behind me.

The rest of the week went by without him mentioning my request. Each time I climbed aboard the bus, in the morning or after school, I looked at him with expectation, wondering if today was the day he'd give me a poem. The following Monday morning, as I got on the bus, he reached into his chest pocket and pulled out a folded piece of paper.

"Here you go," he said, and nodded at me. I was sure I saw a smile within his whiskers.

I said thank you and then found a seat alone. There, I unfolded the page. At the top of the white, unlined sheet of paper, it read: "For Carla Funk." A line underscored my name. Below, in two stanzas that ran the width of the page, black ink leaned forward in cursive, neat as my mother's handwriting.

If you would be happy, then walk with your God,
Through home, and through school, and through life.
He'll guide you, and keep you, and bless your soul,
Through sunshine, through clouds,
                    or through strife.

Just trust in His Mercy, His Grace, and His Love,
As you journey along here below,
And you will find many blessings,
                    —sent down from above,
Which only our God can bestow.

I heard words like *mercy*, *grace*, and *blessings* in Sunday school and in church, but to read them in Mr. Jordan's cursive script, and to see his name—*Frank Jordan*—signed at the bottom and underlined, like my name at the top, made me feel welcomed into a secret club. Frank. *Frank Jordan.* I knew I couldn't say his real name aloud in front of the other bus kids, but out in the schoolyard, as we walked to our coat hooks, I showed the poem to anyone willing to look.

"Frank Jordan wrote it," I said. "Frank Jordan, the bus driver. He wrote it just for me."

I STUDIED FRANK JORDAN'S poem like a schoolbook text. It had two parts, and though I wouldn't have known then to call them stanzas, their shape was clear. Within each section, the end words rhymed. Other words repeated, making echoes in the way the poem sounded when I read it aloud. And in the poem was God.

With a doodle pad and pencil, I sat at the table, writing and crumpling, writing and crumpling.

"What are you drawing?" my mother said.

"I'm not drawing. I'm writing."

The wads of paper around me felt like proof of my work ethic, a sign of how serious were my letters on the page. I wanted my poem to be like Frank Jordan's, but also not like Frank Jordan's. I wanted him to read what I wrote and think of me as different from the other kids on the bus, those loud-mouthed boys, those shrieking girls.

In my neatest printing, with my pencil held steady, I copied out my final draft:

"He's the only one"

He's the only one I want.
He's the only one I have.
He's the only one I would have
if I would choose between a man.

He's the only one there is
to follow day and night.
He's the only one I want
for his name is Jesus Christ.

The next morning, when I boarded Mr. Jordan's bus, I paused at the top of the steps and handed him my folded slip of paper.

"I wrote a poem for you."

I watched him unfold it, scan it, read it, and stood waiting for his response—a look on his face, some sign the words I'd given him were good.

"Thanks," he said, and nodded. He tucked the paper in his chest pocket, cranked closed the bus doors behind me. "Better take your seat."

LESSON BY LESSON, on my typewriter, under the guidance of the instructor's recorded voice, I moved on to words and phrases—*men man map may made many make*—and then into full sentences.

Now is the time for all good men to come to the aid of their party.

Every time Mr. Smith-Corona spoke the words, I echoed them with my fingers, his syllables transposing into the hammer-strike of black ink on crisp white paper.

Now is the time for all good men to come to the aid of their party.

Why the time was *now* and who the men were and what aid they were coming to and why the party needed it and what sort of party anyway—these questions thought-bubbled above me as I typed. I imagined my dad and his truck shop rye-drinking buddies bent around the woodstove for their nightly card game, and a sudden holler from the trees out back, and all of them leaping up from their seats, throwing down their cards, the whole gang running out into the darkness to come to another man's aid, to keep the party going.

152   WHEN I SAW the sign in the window of the Vanderhoof Pharmacy advertising a Father's Day writing contest, I knew it was a sign for me.

Write an essay about your dear old dad and why you love him—and you could win a prize!

"Do you want to enter?" said my mother. "Do you want to write about your father?"

With my fingers rested lightly on the keys, as Mr. Smith-Corona advised, I sat straight-spined, shoulders relaxed, and waited for the first thought. Dear old Dad and why I love him. No baritone voice came to prompt with me with a word.

Now is the time for all good men to come to the aid of their party.
Now is the time for all good men to come to the aid of their party.

My dad hollered down the stairs, wanted to know what all the racket was about, the constant *clack clack clack ding!* coming from the basement.

"I'm writing," I said.

"Huh?" he called.

"Writing!"

I knew that a contest-winning story had to be true and good and full of the right happy elements. I could not write, "My dad had to shoot Grumpy the Saint Bernard because she bit Sparky on the butt," or "Sometimes, if I beg enough, my dad lets me drink beer from his bottle," or "My brother dipped my dad's cigarettes in pee to make him stop smoking so he won't get cancer and die."

I knew I needed to write a story that everyone would want to read, one about a father and a daughter who had adventures together, who liked spending time together. Though the smell inside his logging truck—Export A's and pine air freshener— and the washboard winding gravel roads made me feel like barfing, I imagined myself into a girl who said *yes* when her dad asked if she'd like to go along for a load.

My dad drives a blue Kenworth logging truck. On Saturday mornings, he takes me for a ride to the bush to get a load of logs.

The twisting rutted roads, my queasy gut, the cigarette smoke and dust that filled the cab—I left them off the page, along with the hour we spent waiting our turn while the feller-buncher hacked the trees off their stumps, the skidder dragged them into stacks, and the loader grappled the logs onto the swaying trailers ahead of us in line. I didn't write down my whining about black flies, about boredom, didn't write my dad telling me to quit my gruntzing, get into the truck, and stay out of the way. Instead of everything I didn't love, didn't want, I wrote of how the machines were fun to watch inside that widening clearcut, how they hacked down trees that hit the forest floor with a shudder, then bunched them into bundles for hauling. I wrote of the tiny lady's-slipper orchids that grew wild in the bush, and of how my dad helped me dig them up and bring them home in an empty ice cream bucket for my mother to plant in the patch of dirt beside the fir trees that swayed with our rope swing. How he let me call the miles over the CB radio, naming our distance on the logging road to warn other trucks we were headed their way, and how when we climbed the hill up from the valley, and I said how hungry I was, my dad pulled over at The Blue Spruce to buy me breakfast. How we sat at the table together, me with a stack of silver-dollar pancakes drizzled with syrup, and him with his two fried eggs on toast, yolks running gold over the plate, and he let me sip his coffee, double cream, double sugar, even the final swallow, that silt of sweetness heavy at the bottom of the mug.

ON WEDNESDAY MORNING'S front page, I stared back at myself in black and white. In the photograph, I stood, half-smiling, beside Mr. Stark, the pharmacy manager, and held like trophies the prizes I'd won: a giant stuffed panda with a pink satin bow cinched around its neck, and a gift set of *Gambler* cologne and aftershave, with Kenny Rogers's signature sleekly etched in white ink on the box.

Read inside the winning entry about her dear old logger dad.

My mother flipped the page and scanned the column that bore my name. I watched her face to see how much she knew, what she would read inside the story. I wondered whether she'd show it to my dad, and if he read it, what he would understand—about his daughter, about himself.

My cheeks flushed with heat, the same heat I felt when I unlocked my diary and wrote a slanted version of the truth, words like *I am adopted,* and *I wish I was an orphan,* and *God is angry at me now.* When I read back what I'd writ- ten, I didn't know what to believe—what was real, what was dreamed, and how much to keep secret.

Soon it would be Father's Day. At the breakfast table, while he drank his coffee and smoked his morning cigarette, I'd give him his cologne and aftershave, the box wrapped in shiny paper. As he tore open his gift, he'd say I didn't have to buy him anything, just spending the day together would be enough, a roast-beef Sunday lunch and an afternoon drive up Sinkut Mountain. At the top, we'd climb the steep stairs of the forestry lookout tower and write our names in the visitor log. We'd stand at the high window and survey the world below— Sinkut, Nulki, and Tachick lakes, the Nechako River winding through the valley, the highway leading back to town and curving west, then south, back up the hill toward our house.

Inside, the newspaper lay folded on the kitchen table, my words, in small font and neat columns, spelling out someone else's story, one version of my life as witnessed from a different angle, a view that gave a wider scope. Outside, in the yard, my father's logging truck rumbled into gear, and the air brakes hissed as they let go. Through the frame of the living room window, I watched him drive away into his next shift, heading toward another load to haul, more miles on the radio to call, and the lonely hours until he came back home to me.

All the Ways
to Fall

◇◇◇

ONE IMAGE SHADOWBOXED by memory, one emblem left
open to the touch—that's all it takes to draw me down.
My fingers stray across my forehead, feel the tiny divots,
and the story splits open, spills its colour, scent, and sound.
Like inverse Braille half-hidden in the skin, the scars read
back to me the sunshine glint on the silver rungs, the amber
tang of sawdust, and my dad wagging his "obey me" finger
in my face, his voice growly and curt: *Don't. Don't climb that
ladder.*

"You could get hurt," he said. He held me by the wrist until
I looked him in the eye. "You stay off it. You hear?"

I nodded. I heard. And pulled loose from his grip, a pattern I'd repeat for years to come. My dad in greasy coveralls

squinted up toward the sun and the sound of hammers re-
verberating like shotguns in the open air, then turned back
to his shop, where the air compressor hissed and hours of
monkey-wrenching lay ahead.

The carpenters were halfway through construction of our
new house at the top of the Kenney Dam hill. What had for
months looked like a mud bog, sinkhole, gravel pit, and scrap-
yard was now rising into a two-storey split-level classic. The
gold hue of the new lumber shone. Echoing from the joists
and rafters of what would be the attic floor, hammers on nails
pounded.

Happy to be left alone, I poked around the yard. Always, a
story took shape in this pocket of solitude. Across the property, my mother knelt, pulling chickweed and thistle in the
rototilled dirt of next summer's strawberry patch. Easily I
imagined her into someone else's mom, a stranger who'd take
pity on me, an orphan, lost and starving, surviving on wild
berries and moss as I straggled through the world in search
of home. I plucked a petal from the bloom of an Indian paint-
brush and sucked. That nectar on my tongue—sweet but
scant—was hardly enough to keep me alive, but it would have
to do. Somewhere in the poplar scrub, my brother stalked
with a bow and arrow, tracking grouses. He became my invisible enemy, the shadow stalking me. My pulse kicked up a
notch. In the ditch that bordered the driveway, spring rains
had turned the clay-heavy dirt to a smooth mud. I stamped
my sneakers in it and left a chain of footprints in my wake,
the clues my predator would use to find me, unless someone
swooped down to rescue me first. Past the silver fuel tank on

its stand in the trees, past the trailhead that led to the road, past the sandbox and woodshed, I crept, glancing over my shoulder, making myself afraid of what was coming, until I circled back to where I started, at the far end of the house, and the plot fell away.

Against the side where the chimney had been roughed in, the aluminum ladder leaned. I watched one of the carpenters descend, load the leather pouch on his tool belt with nails from a box on the ground, then climb back up. Every time a steel-toed boot landed on a rung, the ladder shuddered and creaked, but it held. When the man neared the top, he swung his leg up and over the final rungs, shifted to the roof, and disappeared.

When I curled my hand around an eye-level rung, the aluminum surprised me with its heat. My father's words turned and twisted. *Don't climb that ladder* and *you could get hurt* warped to *if you climb* and *don't get hurt*. I tested my foot on the bottom rung. The sole of my sneaker gripped the grooves, and when I reached higher, the foot still touching the ground seemed to follow naturally in response. I knew the Eden story, how God told Eve and Adam, *Eat what you want, just not from this tree growing in the middle of the garden*. Every time I heard about how sin came into the world, I saw Eve reaching out to pluck that rosy fruit, and wanted to crash the scene and slap her hand away, yell for her to stop, *don't do it, don't listen to the snake*. That devil-serpent sliding in the grass, weaving up the tree trunk, circling Eve's shoulder like a sneaky necklace was trickery, and still she fell for the charm and hiss, bit in, swallowed, and passed the poison on.

I was halfway up before my father's voice came back again—
don't climb, distant and dim, more whisper than warning. I
looked back across the yard, toward the shop, which seemed
so far away and smaller now from where I stood. My dad was
gone, in greasy coveralls beneath a truck, invisible, unseeing.
I only wanted to see what the carpenters could see, what the
world looked like from their lofty vantage. I'd make it up the
ladder and down again before he noticed.

Once I reached the final rungs, I swung myself over the top
and off the ladder, half-crawling on my belly until the surface
beneath me was solid and flat. In front of me, two ballcapped,
tool-belted men knelt. Around them, tools. A level, a hammer,
a silver square. Handsaws and tape measures. From the centre of the roof, a portable radio with an angled silver antenna
chattered news. The man closest to me wore dark glasses and
had a flat, wide pencil tucked behind his ear. His face, when
I stood up, lifted to meet mine with a look of surprise, but he
smiled, friendly enough, and thinking that I might walk to
the end of the roof and back, I took a step toward him.

From that high up, I could see our full five acres—the
tractor-tilled garden plot, the rust-red pigpen, the clearcut of
stumps, and the birch and poplar trees beyond. The landscape
stretched out wide and far, but from my higher station, the
world and its inhabitants looked small. My brother, a rustling
in the bushes. My mother, only a dot of blue and white amid
the brown. My father, the whirr of machinery and work drifting from across the property.

Whenever my mother chided me with the proverb about
how *pride goeth before a fall*, I pictured the Looney Tunes

cliff edge with its wide-eyed coyote scrabbling for traction, a joke in which the predator becomes the punchline, and everyone laughs because the villain gets what's coming to him. Before I had even taken a second step forward on that roof, the foreman jumped to his feet and held out his hand like a crossing guard signalling *stop*, knowing what was about to happen, seeing what I couldn't see—that where the chimney flue had been roughed in, an opening in the roof remained, half-covered by a sheet of plywood, but with enough room left for a girl my size to slip right through. Down on air, surprised by gravity, I fell.

From a great height. From grace. On stony ground. Flat on my face. To my knees, to pieces. All the ways to fall tumbled with me, around me, in me. The word itself cracked open, first utterance of the plunge from glory, light to dark. One moment I stood bathed in sunshine, thrilling to my new high place. Though I couldn't see as far as the future, all those coming falls—scorch of whisky from the bottle, bedroom window sliding open like a secret, cigarette haloes on a stranger's front lawn, first taste of his mouth, other mouths—flickered, flashes of how I'd try to leave the low-level view of the world, find a shaky rung and climb. I saw enough to know how height can feel like power. When I plummeted to blackout, that fall, like every fall, was a falling both forward and back, the story throwing out its hitch to hook me, the apple not far from the tree.

I woke up stumbling on rocks. Beneath my feet, the shifting crush of gravel made it hard to walk. My chest hurt, like when I had tried to turn a backflip on the trampoline and landed on my head, my neck bent back, the wind knocked out. I lurched forward, blood in my eye. My arm dangled like pins-and-needles asleep, stinging. My shoulder burned.

The foreman found me in the framed-up basement, crying, looking for an exit. Perhaps because he was a father with a daughter only a few years older than me, he scooped me up, held me like a baby in his arms. Every step of his jog across the yard lolled my head and made the pain rattle and stab. He yelled my father's name, my mother's name, called out, *Hey! Hey!* And though my eyes were swelling shut, I saw it all, like a movie, in flashes, from far away and overhead, but with the soundtrack dialed down. Voices and faces blurred to under-water sounds. My mom rising from the garden, her white sun hat falling to the dirt, her hands over her mouth. Then my dad, rushing out of the shop in his coveralls, wiping his hands on a grease rag. He throws open the pickup side door, and my brother flies from the bushes and scrambles over the tailgate into the box, pressing himself against the open rear window. I'm cradled in arms. I'm floating overhead, hovering like in my dreams of flight.

Faster, my mother said, *drive.* I lay across the bench seat, my head in her lap. The rev of the gas pedal gunned us down the hill toward town. The crackle of my father's CB radio and his voice cutting into it, calling out to a passing logging truck that we were heading to emergency. Tire squeal on the corner at the light, my father's name, sirens, the idling engine, and through the open window, another man's voice, and my dad saying, *Kid's had an accident.* Then the gas pedal, wind rushing from the open windows, and sirens all the way down the main drag, across the bridge, up the hospital hill.

The scissor blades slid cold across my chest. The doctor, his face hovering over me, told me to hold still as he cut away my T-shirt—the new one, red and white and blue with stripes. Hem to collar, the T-shirt with the lace-up front, the one I'd learned to tie with a bow at the top, fell open, fell to pieces, then flew from the doctor's hand to the garbage can in the corner of the room.

"You'll have to keep her head from moving," said the nurse. A black cloth fell over my face, and then again, cold scissors, snipping above my eye so that a slit of light came through.

My mother said, "Pinch my arm. Pinch as hard as you can"—her code for *this is going to hurt*. The needle in my forehead like a wasp, a fleck of hot ash. I kicked the air, gripped my mother's forearm, her skin between my thumb and finger pinched so tight, the welt remained a week.

On the gurney, I lay beneath a paper sheet as the doctor hooked the suture needle into my forehead and tied off stitches in a jagged row. My favourite T-shirt, gone. My pants, pulled off and rolled up in my mother's purse. My hair, matted and crusted with dirt and blood. Dazed beneath the overhead surgical lights, I sat up, hunched, as hands fitted a halter brace around my torso and cinched it tight to hold my broken collarbone in place.

WHEN MY MOTHER held me up to the mirror above our bathroom sink, a stranger looked back. A girl with two black eyes nearly swollen shut, and above the left brow, a line of stitches.

Dried blood streaked the cheekbones, scraped by rebar jutting from the chimney's cinderblock. I couldn't look away from her, that other self that peered back at me, proof I'd earned it all, that the fault was mine. I'd heard my dad say to my mother, *I told her to stay off*, their voices tense in the brightness of the room.

For days, I lay on the chesterfield in an undershirt and pajama bottoms, humiliated by the neighbourhood moms and kids who showed up with gifts and get-well-soon cards. Uncles and aunts and cousins stopped by, too, to hear my dad recount the story. He never tired of telling how he had warned me not to climb the ladder, and then he dragged a vertical drop in the air with his finger—*fffsh*—down the chimney I went. Someone always cracked a Christmas joke—"You trying to play Santa Claus?" Someone always said, "Good thing the fire wasn't burning."

"Show them," my dad said, pulling back the blanket. He pointed out my stitches, cuts, and scrapes as if to testify to how hard and far I'd fallen. I turned away and sulked into the cushions until my mother said, "Okay, enough."

My bruises morphed from black to lilac to green to sallow gold. The wounds on my cheeks scabbed over and began to fade. The doctor drew the halter tighter, but still, the broken collarbone felt wrong. For weeks, I lay around the house trying not to move. The pain in my shoulder throbbed when I breathed too deeply. When I moved in my sleep, I woke crying. My mother pressed her cheek to my forehead to check for fever, held a straw to my lips so I could drink my apple juice.

"Take her to Mrs. Giesbrecht," my dad said. "She'll fix her up."

IN THE MENNONITE community, Mrs. Giesbrecht was the one to see when your body wasn't working, especially if the doctors couldn't help. With her man-sized hands, she knew how to turn a breech baby, set a bone, align a spine, and unsnarl a knotted muscle—a *gnerpl*. Everything she knew she had learned by practice, like the old midwives who apprenticed at the bedside instead of in the classroom. Everyone called her a "care-o-practor," and no one cared that she had no medical certificate or diploma hanging on her wall.

She met us at the front door, quiet-voiced and smiling. She was a sturdy woman with large, thick glasses, who wore her brown-grey hair in a tight bun at the top of her head, slicked and piled up and held together with a nest of bobby pins. Most middle-aged Mennonite women wore simple dresses and head coverings, but Mrs. Giesbrecht wore dark slacks and a flowered blouse. After a few words with my mother, she led us through the living room, where the curtains were drawn and her husband sat in front of the TV, staring at the screen. The whole house was dim, small, closed in, and the narrow hallway down which we followed her seemed to grow darker as we walked.

On a table covered with a quilt and a bedsheet, I lay on my back while Mrs. Giesbrecht rubbed liniment oil on her hands, the smell like hospital and sickness. She started on my shoulder, feeling along my arm, my ribs, then my neck. My mother sat on the edge of a bed tucked against the wall, holding on to her purse, telling Mrs. Giesbrecht about the fall. Mrs. Giesbrecht nodded, said, *Yo*, she understood. Though her hands pressed my shoulder, pulled my arm across my chest, nothing hurt. She spoke in Low German while she worked, in the kind of voice the grey-haired women used at prayer meetings. My mother sat quiet in the background, as if in a dream, there and not there, and I floated in that threshold space between waking and sleep, my limbs heavy and yet hollow, Mrs. Giesbrecht's voice murmuring familiar sounds but no words I understood.

Then *yes, oh but yo, that is it*, Mrs. Giesbrecht said, and her hands tightened on my shoulder, stretching and turning, a pain now, but different than the stab and ache—this time like orange easing into yellow into white, and then as if fitting together a notch into a groove, she shifted my collarbone with one clean, quick maneuver. What the fall had broken in me, she fixed, setting right the off-kilter part that wouldn't heal inside, my body malleable as mud in her hands. When I sat up and drew in a breath, my rib cage didn't burn, my shoulder didn't throb. Mrs. Giesbrecht pulled my sleeve back over my shoulder, and my mother stood up, fished in her purse, and handed her a twenty-dollar bill, payment for my back-room healing, however small the miracle.

AS SPRING SHIFTED into summer, we moved into the new house. Because the main floor wasn't yet finished with carpets and flooring and paint, we lived in the basement through the first winter. Where months earlier I'd stumbled over crushed rock and staggered through the lumber framework, we now ate our meals, watched TV, practiced piano, bathed, slept. In the living room, every time I watched my mother kneel at the fireplace with kindling and crumpled newspaper, strike a wooden match, and send smoke rolling up that chimney, I saw myself falling all over again. Falling through darkness, falling into flames. Climbing charred from the hearth like some girl out of myth. "It could have been worse," my mother always said. "It could have been so much worse."

When I climbed that silver ladder to the sky, I knew that what I was doing was wrong, and because it was wrong, I wanted to do it. The old story's forbidden thrill that lay coiled up inside me asked to be fed, wanted to be tasted. My father's voice saying *no*, saying *don't*, made me crave the *yes* and *why not*. The voice that urged me rung by rung toward the roof was deep down in me, I knew it, a little hiss that tendrilled from the heart of me, the same whisper that slipped me hints and missives. *Sneak another lemon drop*, when my mother turned her back. *It wasn't really you who ripped the page. You don't know how it happened, how the teacup cracked, why the clock fell off the wall.* The climb and fall cut in me a promise of more to come. More stitches, more scars. More of the laying on of hands in future rooms, in darkness. More of me rising from the bed, from the dirt. And more of me waiting to be set right, made new.

Sunday Dad

◇◇◇

GONE WERE THE cigarette smoke, burnt coffee, and my dad's grease-stained work clothes. Gone the week day incense that hung its cloud throughout the house. Instead of him sitting at the dining room table working through a stack of pink load slips, punching the buttons on his adding machine to tally the logs hauled and money owing, and puffing a smoke haze toward the light fixture, he sat with us, fully awake, fully present. He wore polyester slacks with a sharp crease ironed down the front of each leg and a crisp dress shirt with its top two buttons undone, the collar spread open to reveal the clean white T-shirt beneath.

At the table on Sunday mornings, we sat together, passing platters of pancakes and bacon and hash browns like a family on holiday and feasting. Even the radio's gospel hour harmonized with us. Though in the hour before church my dad might yet change his mind about coming with us, I watched with hope for signs of life. If in his left chest pocket he carried dinner mints instead of a pack of Export A's, if he splashed on extra aftershave, if he ran his comb through his slicked-back hair one more time, chances were high we'd be on our way, all four of us together in the shiny green Chrysler, revving down the hill and into the valley.

In the driver's seat with the window cocked, my dad drove with one hand on the steering wheel, and with the other, tapped the dashboard in time to the beat of the music on his favourite 8-track tape. When Ferlin Husky sang "On the Wings of a Dove," and the rising melody flew us across the wooden bridge that spanned the river, if my dad hummed along with the chorus, I knew that day he'd join us in our wooden pew at the back of the sanctuary.

When we walked through the double doors of the church, the deacons who stood inside the foyer to welcome con-gregants acted as if my dad were a special celebrity guest. Even the pastor beelined toward him and shook his hand for what seemed like a long time, clasping his shoulder as he pumped that handshake, asking how the logging was going, how bush camp was treating him, *how's the family, good to see you, so very good to have you here.* My mother whisked off to hang up our coats, leaving my dad to stand with his brothers and talk truck, all of them in a row with their arms folded across their chests, looking straight ahead, all of them sucking on mints until the church buzzer buzzed to signal the start of service, and my mother led us to our pew.

Mr. Rempel, the tall, bald man with glasses as thick as my dad's, took the pulpit and welcomed us again to the house of the Lord. "Turn for our opening hymn," he said, "to number 248, 'When the Roll is Called Up Yonder.'" As the piano and vibraphone played the opening chords, my dad flipped the pages of the hymnal, licking his thumb to get a grip on the paper, searching as if lost. When finally he found the right song, the congregation was halfway through the first verse. He held the book low so my brother and I could see the notes and words, and together, we launched into the chorus. My mother, holding her own hymnal, carried the soprano melody. My dad's voice was strained, an almost-tenor holding its pitch, singing about *that bright and cloudless morning when the dead in Christ shall rise*. As he sang, the Scotch mint clacked against his molars. Every few minutes, he reached into his shirt pocket and plucked out another, popped it into his mouth. When we swung back again into the chorus, repeating the words *when the roll is called up yonder*, I pictured the hill beside Grandma Funk's house and one of her giant homemade buns inflated to the size of a car rolling up that gravelled slope that led to the auto junkyard—the roll, being called up yonder to the open field of scrap metal and rusted-out wrecks. *When the roll is called up yonder I'll be there*, the congregation sang in four-part harmony, my dad's foot tapping to the marching cut-time rhythm.

To be this close to him, the sleeve of my dress touching the sleeve of his shirt, made church feel like a special occasion, like Baptism Sunday with its row of congregants kneeling at the front, waiting for the silver pitcher to pour a stream of water on their bowed heads, or Easter Sunday with its potted lilies lining the edge of the stage, and the call and response of the congregation standing to echo the preacher's procla-

170 mation of *He is risen!* After worship, when we sat down, my dad handed us each a mint and then offered his hands, one for my brother to hold and one for me. With his palm up on my lap, I picked away his calluses, tugging the edges of the hardened yellow skin until a thread came loose. While the preacher read aloud another parable of the Kingdom—the rocky ground, the scattered sheep, the prodigal son chewing on a corncob in a pigpen instead of feasting with his father, we worked our dad's hands, peeling away their leathery toughness. By the time we stood for "Blest Be the Tie That Binds," the final benediction, the rough and sallow calluses had given way to soft pink flesh, and on the carpet at our feet, the bits of old skin lay.

Where his mind drifted while we sat together in that pew and what he heard inside the sermons, I never considered. When the preacher told the story of the rich young ruler who knelt at Jesus's feet and said, *What must I do to follow you?* I pictured my dad in the middle of the driveway with the rolled-up bay doors of his shop behind him, his new Kenworth gleaming and ready for another load, and Jesus standing in front of him, saying, *Forsake it all.* The truck, the shop, the fridge full of whisky, and the Kal Tire calendar's summer beach bikini girls—he could never give them up.

WHETHER IT WAS the preacher's message on tithing—about how God commanded people to give money no matter how rich or poor—or his stern words about the perils and pitfalls of alcohol, fornication, and gambling, I still don't know, but by the time I was five, my dad had quit church.

"Monkey-wrenching to do," he'd say, or, "Someone's gotta split the firewood if you yahoos aren't here."

Not much was said about it out in the open, but I had the sense that the muffled conversations happening behind the locked bedroom door every Sunday morning had something to do with his refusal to attend. At family gatherings, Grandma Funk would look with her kind, watery eyes across the table at my dad, her firstborn child, and say things like, "Oh, bah, it would be good for you to come again." Grandpa Funk said nothing. My dad looked away, crossed his arms, and leaned back in his chair, his jaw clenching and unclenching.

Some of the Sunday ritual held on to my dad, though, even after he stopped coming to services. He still sat down with us for a proper after-church lunch and took his nap like he always did, sleeping off Saturday's late night and the morning's work on the chesterfield. In the late afternoon, my mother clicked on the TV for *Hymn Sing*, the half-hour show in which a small choir of men and women in matching robes sang the old hymns in four-part harmony. My dad yawned, let his false teeth slide loose from his mouth and perch half-in, half-out. His hair, no longer slicked back into a ducktail, fluffed up in flyaway strands. Without his glasses, he saw only blurred shapes and shadows.

"Mom," he called to me, mistaking my identity. "What time is it?" My dad fumbled on the end table for his glasses, fitted them back to the miracle of sight, and sat on the edge of the couch cushion until he got his bearings.

"Almost Tommy Hunter time," I said.

The Tommy Hunter Show was my dad's all-time favourite, better even than *Wild Kingdom* or *Fandango*, the country-music quiz show he watched on weekend afternoons when he wasn't hauling logs. As the theme music and opening credits ran, the regular cast—Leroy and Donna, the house band, and Tommy—flashed on the screen with white-toothed smiles and glinting eyes, and after that day's special guests were announced, Tommy himself jogged out in a leather vest and bolo tie, carrying his guitar. He welcomed his studio audience, saluted the viewers in TV land, then took his place centre stage behind the microphone and broke into the first rousing song.

Tommy knew how to keep it light and jokey with his fellow stars for the first half of the show, but after the second commercial break, he shifted into a mellow, tenderhearted mood. The penultimate number always featured Tommy half-standing, half-sitting on a stool, bathed in soft light with a stained-glass window behind him. This was the point where my dad leaned toward the screen with the same attention he gave the Wednesday-night Lotto 6/49 draw. When Tommy recited a poem or told a story, my father looked as though he were the only one being spoken to. His gaze stayed locked on Tommy, and the rest of us in the room faded to background noise. Tommy's voice dropped low when the old horse's swayback gave way beneath the cowboy, surged when the flames of a barn fire blazed out of control, and gentled to an *amen* and *God bless y'all* at the end. If Tommy had been our church's preacher, my dad surely would have listened to every verse and sermon, would maybe even have heeded the final altar call, rising from his pew to make his way down to the front of the sanctuary while the organ played "Just As I Am," the classic hymn of repentance and surrender.

"That Tommy's a good guy," my dad said, as if he knew him. "Canada's country gentleman."

Sometimes, Tommy's closing number was a familiar hymn, his country take on "I Come to the Garden Alone" or "Will the Circle Be Unbroken," songs my dad knew well, songs with enough ache and longing to send him rummaging in the dining room junk drawer. "Where's the mouth organ?" he wanted to know, and when he found the hinged cardboard box, he sat back down in front of the TV, pulled out the harmonica he had bought as a young man, and ran his mouth back and forth over the holes in a sliding scale. While the closing credits rolled, he found his starting note and breathed out the only songs he knew—the chorus of "Jingle Bells," no matter the season, and "Jesus Loves Me."

He cupped the harmonica, humming through his hands, his fingers yellowed and creased with the work and dirt of the week behind him. I sat beside him on the edge of the couch, listening to him feel his way through a refrain I sang every Sunday with the children's choir in the basement of the church, his song wordless, but carrying pieces of a tune we both knew by heart.

The Pledge

◇◇◇

I PLEDGE
My HEAD to clearer thinking,
My HEART to greater loyalty,
My HANDS to larger service,
My HEALTH to better living,
For my club, my community, and my country.
—THE 4-H PLEDGE

"THE WHOLE THING reminds me of the Moonies," said my mother on the drive home from my first 4-H Club meeting. She still shook her head over that day a young, long-haired woman had wormed her way into our house and sold us a huge decorative candle. "I'm raising funds that will build our church," she told my mother, who eyed her warily from across the living room. The candle woman talked softly about the Unification Church and the Reverend Moon, the man she called True Father, the one who who'd lead them into abundant love and life after death. The experience of the Moonie woman sitting in our house for two hours talking about unity and the Four Position Foundation and humanity's liberation from sin, together with the monstrous ten-dollar candle she'd been coerced into buying, had left my mother suspicious that cult activity was going on all around us and in unsuspected places. The candle, whorled and swirled in shades of brown with ornamental cut-outs in the wax, was still displayed atop a doily on one of our living room end tables, and every Friday afternoon, when my mother ran her dusting cloth over the furniture, she picked up the candle and wondered aloud why she hadn't thrown it away. *Pffft, those Moonies*, she'd say, then set the candle back down and move along to the coffee table.

"I don't like the way you have to put your hand on your heart when you pledge," my mother said, gripping the steering wheel, shaking her head. "That's weird."

We bumped along the rutted gravel roads of the rural farming district way beyond the town limits, heading home. In the cold and drafty community hall where the meeting was held, I'd sat for an hour on a wooden chair, one in a row of kids who all wanted to raise livestock. We listened to a man in denim overalls talk about the importance of good citizenship, what it meant to be a young leader in today's world, and how, like the Club motto preached, "to make the better best." In 4-H, said the man, you'll learn to do by doing. You'll raise an animal. You'll groom it. You'll practice good stewardship. And if you work hard, you'll even make some money.

Most of the club members came from true farming families. They already knew how to brand a steer, rope a calf, shear a sheep, saddle a horse, and slash a knife into a cow's belly to let out the bloat. But I was a newcomer, there because the two neighbour girls had decided to join, and when I heard they'd be raising lambs as their 4-H project, I needed a lamb, too.

"I'll do all the work," I promised my parents. "I'll clean up after it. Feed it. You won't have to do a thing."

After a week of daily begging, pleading my 4-H case at the breakfast table, the dinner table, spouting off facts about lambs and the gentleness of the Suffolk cross breed—good for its wool *and* its meat!—pointing out that while we had pigs and chickens, a dog and a cat, and a hamster running frantically in its wire wheel, we most certainly did not have a lamb, had never had a lamb, and that seemed wrong. My dad was the one who caved first. A sucker for any animal, he liked the idea of a lamb.

"Fried chop with some mint and garlic," he said. "I like that."

I helped him clear out the old red shed, hauling rusty truck parts and lumber scraps away to make room for a stall. While my dad sawed and hammered, I handed him nails, the level, the measuring tape, doing what he asked without complaint, a rare state of peace between us as we worked. Like the *Lamb Raising Handbook* instructed, I raked sawdust over the floorboards and spread bales of fresh straw at one end for bedding. I set out the salt lick, the water bucket, and a trough for the grain and hay.

As I surveyed the clean, still-empty stall, I believed the true and perfect version of the story, in which I rose every morning to greet and feed my lamb, brush the dirt from its fleece, lead it around the yard in wide circles to simulate the judging ring, and teach it to stand in proper position, all four feet squared and rear legs slightly back, as outlined in the *Market Lamb Showmanship Guide*. In this version of the story, we won grand champion, and I ended up with money in my hand, a lamb beside me, and a fat blue ribbon that drew the praise and envy of the other 4-H-ers who thronged around me, clapping, wishing they were me.

ON A SPRING Saturday when the world was in full thaw, the snow in scraps and the ice running into puddles, I stood on the perimeter of the livestock barn with a group of kids, kicking at the packed sawdust and manure. We waited like team captains ready to choose draft picks. A flock of black-faced, white-wooled lambs huddled together, bleating for their mothers. Each Suffolk cross had a number spray-painted in red on its fleece. The 4-H leader, holding his clipboard and pen, read off our names, and each of us in turn stepped forward to select a lamb.

My dad stood on the other side of the barn gate, and when my turn came to choose, he called out to me.

"That one," he said, pointing. "Number 47. He's a big guy."

Number 47 was the loudest in the flock, too, and, as it turned out, hard to catch, but finally, after he slipped my grip, and after a brief chase and gambol, a team of three teenagers corralled the lamb in a corner and slid a collar around his neck. I clipped on a rope leash, and Number 47 was mine.

I rode home in the back of the pickup box, cold wind in my face and hair, rattling over the gravel road and clutching the lamb that struggled to get away from me, to slip its collar, to choke me with the rope. With every mile, my grip on the kicking creature tightened. My heart cinched, too. The sweet-faced lamb's whimpering bleat had deepened to a crackly *baa* that sounded like my gout-struck great-grandfather's chronic cough. After all the pleading I'd done, the begging, the vowing and pleading—*I'll take care of it, I'll be responsible, sheep are my favourite animal ever!*—I couldn't admit my gut-sick dread. It was the same feeling I had whenever I got stuck holding a baby and its mother left the room. *Come back*, I'd plead with my eyes, *don't leave me here alone, in charge*.

Once we were home, my dad popped the tailgate and hauled down the lamb, which was by this point bellowing.

"He wants his mom," my dad said.

I wanted my mom, too. I wanted her to swoop in and tell me she'd take over from here, that I should just go inside and watch cartoons. But instead, she headed for the house, leaving my dad and me alone with Number 47.

My dad leaned on the stall fence, puffing on a cigarette, looking in. I sat down in the corner of the stall on a clean pile of hay and waited for 47 to come lie down beside me. Instead, he stood at the gate, bawling his gout sound, staring at my dad.

"What're you gonna call him?" my dad said.

The lamb bleated louder. He couldn't be Number 47 forever. I tried out names on him—*Bubba, Bob, Marvin*—calling to see which one he answered to.

"Nope," said my dad.

Rocky. The lamb stopped hollering and nosed the grain in the wooden trough, then peed a steaming stream into the sawdust. That was sign enough for me.

"Rocky," my dad said, "come here." He shifted his cigarette to his mouth and held out his hand through the slats of the fence.

Rocky blinked his long, black eyelashes and nosed my dad's fingers. From where I sat in the stall, the fresh straw smell had already begun to shift toward stench.

THOSE FIRST FEW weeks, I wanted him gone. I wanted to rewind my life and put Rocky back in the flock as Number 47, to let someone else choose him. I wanted to undo the thing I'd done, to be the girl who visited the 4-H lambs next door but who didn't have one of her own. The neighbour girls adored their lambs, Josie and Amy, and gushed about the way they nuzzled their necks and nibbled the cuffs of their jeans.

Daily, I collared Rocky and led him to the grass to graze, tethering him to a picket line so he could cruise in a circle in the backyard. I brushed the sawdust, bugs, and dirt from his wool. I followed the rules of 4-H animal husbandry, checking his hooves and eyes and rump and teeth for any signs of illness. As the *Lamb Raising Handbook* suggested, I spent quality time with my livestock, trying to form a bond and earn my animal's trust and affection. I sat inside the stall on the salt lick with a stack of Archie comics, waiting for Rocky to nuzzle me, but instead, he head-butted my knee and, when I pushed him away, tried to mount my back, his hooves scraping when he reared.

"He's lonely," said my mother.

"He's frisky," said my dad. "Let him go for a run."

"He'll run away," I said, panicked, and then the bright side of those words flickered. *He'll run away*, I thought, and started to imagine how I could blame my dad, say it was his fault—he was the one who opened the stall, he let Rocky go free, and now my lamb was gone, and I had no lamb, and *I'm sorry, but I'm not part of 4-H anymore.* I already saw myself crying in the empty stall, holding Rocky's old rope and collar. *I loved that lamb.*

My dad unlatched the stall door and let it swing wide. Before I could grab Rocky, he bolted out the gate and frisked up the driveway, across the yard, trotting for the front lawn and through my mother's flowerbeds, trampling the marigolds and pansies, kicking his hooves in full frolic as he went. I ran to the grass with my rope, calling his name, heart rate rising, expecting a chase and failure, but at my voice, Rocky lifted his head, turned, and trotted back to me. He stopped in front of me, nudged my hand with his nose, then plucked a mouthful of clover and started chewing, his lower jaw working circles to break down the cud. I sat on the lawn and let him sniff me, nibble at my hair with his velvet-bristled lips, his breath like sweetgrass in my face.

EVERYTHING WE DID in the program, the projects and pledging, demonstration days and educational workshops, was building toward the Fall Fair, our town's annual agricultural exhibition. There, we'd all show our animals in the judging ring, and on the final day, lead them into the arena for the 4-H auction. I knew in theory what this meant—that Rocky, like every lamb, steer, and hog, would end, but this head-knowledge remained abstract and distant, a paragraph in the club handbook, a far-off date on the calendar.

At Rally Day, our final club event before the Fair, I stood in gumboots in an outdoor pen with my fellow members, holding my tiny pencil and judging card. We were there to learn how to assess lambs for what our handbook called their "market value."

The leader of Rally Day was a short, muscular man named Jim, the dad of one of the other 4-H kids. He wore the uniform of a rancher—blue jeans, a Western shirt, and a cowboy hat cocked to shadow his eyes. When he began to speak, we leaned in to hear his brusque instructional.

"The ideal lamb." He hooked his thumbs in his belt loops and cleared his throat. "Is deep and wide." He walked over to one of the demonstration animals tethered to the fence. "Low-set." He grabbed the lamb around the midsection and squeezed. "Not excessively fat." The lamb made a sound like a toy with a broken squeaker. "But roomy. The ribs well-sprung."

A ram, he explained, needs to show ruggedness, and a ewe should be refined in her features.

None of what he said made any sense to me. The lambs all looked the same—dirty white bodies, black faces and legs. I liked the ones that stood vacantly chewing their cud, quiet and unfazed by the buzzing flies. On the card I had been handed, bold letters at the top spelled "Cuts of a Market Lamb." Below the title, an ink drawing showed the lamb's body sectioned into six main parts, each part divided by a dotted line. My task was to first label the cuts—leg, loin, rib, shoulder, breast, foreshank—and then to rank the four lambs in order of highest market value.

The other kids appeared to understand what our Rally Day leader meant and set to work scrutinizing the animals, squeezing rib cages, digging their fingers into fleece, peeling back lips, inspecting teeth, palpating rumps. I walked behind and mimicked their actions, but to me, the ideal sheep was the one without any dried manure clumped around its tail. When Jim announced the true ranking, my lowest-ranked lamb—the clumpy-butted one with eye gunk and thick loins—was at the top, and the one I'd chosen as the champion was second from the bottom, substandard, lacking in form and frame. Rocky, it seemed, was somewhere in the middle, not ideal, but good enough, said Jim, to garner a fair price for his poundage.

LATE AUGUST, THE fairgrounds on the outskirts of the town—normally a scattering of vacant outbuildings and empty riding rings—came to life. In the exhibition hall, long tables held the various offerings of participants. Quilters hung their hand-stitched quilts. Bakers brought their best baked bread, pies, cookies, cakes. Glass jars gleamed with jellies and jams in every flavour—huckleberry, gooseberry, strawberry, saskatoon. Pumpkins, tomatoes, potatoes, cabbage—every vegetable vied for the blue ribbon in garden produce. Kids entered creatures made out of vegetables, pencil-crayoned portraits of indiscernible family members, hand-sewn doll clothes for their Cabbage Patch Kids. Beyond the exhibition hall, every shed, barn, and stall held a horse or steer, a cage of rabbits or clutch of hens, a pink, washed hog.

After three days on the fairgrounds, with Rocky in his own stall inside the sheep barn, a participation ribbon tacked on the wall above him, I knelt in the dirt and sawdust of the auction arena with my one arm around Rocky's neck and the other over his back, facing the bleachers full of bidders. Behind me on a small stage stood the auctioneer, a man in a Stetson, leather vest, and bolo tie. He let loose a string of syllables that sounded less like dollar amounts and more like a foreign tongue. In the stands, a cowboy nodded his head, to which the auctioneer responded by pointing, then climbing a notch in pitch and price: *I have a dollar ten, wouldyougoadollartwenty, dollartwenty, bidonadollartwenty, I wannadollartwenty.*

My dad, behind the arena fence and at the top of the bleachers, sat hunched with his arms crossed and elbows on his knees. Every time another cowboy or trucker or 4-H father bid on Rocky, he answered with a bid of his own, leap-frogging the winning bidder, then falling behind, then raising the bid again.

As I held on to Rocky in the auction arena and watched my father tip his ballcap, lift his raised thumb as a signal to take up the bid a notch, and as I heard the price per pound rise in ten-cent increments, then five-cent increments, I felt the truth come on hard. Rocky was stepping into the pattern of every 4-H lamb that came before him. He was a living, bleating version of the pen-and-ink illustration on the Rally Day judging card. I saw in my mind's eye the stark outline overlaid on him, superimposed in dotted lines marking the loin, the shoulder, the choice cuts of a market lamb.

"Sold to the man in the blue hat," Charlie the auctioneer announced, and pointed at my dad in his top-row bleacher seat.

My world blurred—kneeling beside Rocky in the ring, the winning bid, my dad making his way down the stairs toward me, wallet in hand, ready to fill in the dollars and sign his name on a cheque. He looked pleased, proud to have won the bid. A faint hope flickered in me—the brief thought that he bought Rocky off the auction block so that I might keep him as a pet. I saw the alternate version—the ride home from the fair, the return to the empty stall, the hanging up of the rope leash and collar, the grain spilled out into the trough, and Rocky weathering through autumn, winter, spring, summer, then set free to frolic in the green world.

"Got you a better price," said my dad.

I couldn't look him in the eye. I knew the story's end. I'd read it in the plain type of the club handbook. My hands had worked that checklist to code, mucking out the stalls, pitch-forking new straw, grooming, pledging myself to *clearer thinking, greater loyalty, larger service, better living.* All along, my head was telling my heart to keep the gate latched, but ritual had turned somehow to allegiance, to affection, to a vague, shaky version of love.

It was as if my dad had been planning it all along, standing at both ends of the story, choosing Number 47 as a future freezer full of meat wrapped in brown butcher paper and portioned into stewing cubes, chops, racks, and roasts. What my dad intended for my good—a profit on the price per pound—felt like a hot slap on the cheek.

I made my way out of the arena, across the trail of sawdust and back to the sheep barn. I climbed into the stall with Rocky and buried my face in his neck. He smelled like a hot wool blanket left out on a bed of wet grass and manure, a scent that those first weeks had turned my stomach. Now, as Rocky chewed his wad of cud, I cried fat tears over what felt like a bad joke with a sorry punchline, a trick ending to my pledge. Soon, I'd join the sad parade of 4-H kids, all of us leading our lambs out of the barn's back entrance to where the big white truck idled with the ramp down, waiting to haul away the flock. On the other side of the fairground fence, my dad would be watching with the other parents, lifting his cigarette in a half-wave at me, smiling over how it all turned out.

SUMMER

Barbecue, Baptism

◇◇◇

ALL OUR BEST stories had blood.

In the firelight of Grandpa and Grandma Shenk's living room, where I sat with my cousins at Uncle Glen's feet, listening to him tell again of the lumber mill accident, I waited for it—the hit, the heat, the rush of blood.

"I was nineteen years old," Uncle Glen said, "and working the night shift." He perched on the hearth and leaned down toward us, his voice low and hushed.

"My job was tailing the small edger, hey? I was separating the boards as they came down the belt, taking off the scrap wood as it came down my chain and sending the good wood down to the stacker. I was just working away, when—*bam*—my glove caught."

The pain, he said, was like a shot from a nail gun through his hand. He tried to pull his glove free from where it was pinched between the rollers, but that glove was wedged tight. He pulled hard, so hard his hand came out of the glove, but then blood came too—running down his arm and spattering the sawdust-covered concrete.

Uncle Glen held up his ragged hand and called, "My finger—where's my finger?"

One of the guys on the chain hit the emergency stop, and while Uncle Glen sat dizzy on the ground with his bleeding hand raised above his head, the crew searched through the pile of boards. Sure enough, caught in the rollers among the boards was the lost glove, and inside that glove, his little finger curled, pink as a baby shrew.

The mill's medic drove him to the hospital, where he lay sweating on a gurney, staring at the severed and whitening finger in its bowl of ice. Three hours later, when the doctor finally showed up, it was too late for the pinkie to be sewn back on.

"The doctor sewed me up," said Uncle Glen, "and threw the torn finger in the trash."

And here, like every time he told the story, he held up his left hand with its nub of a pinkie and waggled the remaining fingers.

Does it still hurt, we wanted to know, and how much.

"Nope," he said, "but the itch about drove me crazy for years." He scratched at the space where his finger used to be. "Phantom finger. Even now I sometimes can feel it."

Uncle Glen offered us his hand, and we took turns touching it, feeling the bump of bone and skin, like the start of a finger or its end, rubbing the callus of scar tissue where the doctor had stitched it shut.

All our best stories had blood, as if the blood was what fuelled them and gave them their heart. Blood was proof of the trouble we had in this world, proof that trouble hurt, and would always find a way to leave its mark on us. Though *mortality* was a word not yet in my vocabulary, I had the sense that somehow blood told the truth. It flowed from inside the body and held the body's secrets. Death—and the threat of it—made me lean in, not only with the heart-thud thrill of fear, but with curiosity about what came next. Even the Bible stories I loved most had blood, injury, and danger, like the story of Jael, the woman who snuck into the tent where the enemy soldier slept and drove a tent peg through his skull, or the tale of Samson the strong man with his eyes gouged out, or the one about Shadrach, Meshach, and Abednego, the Israelite men thrown into the fiery furnace for refusing to bow to an idol of the king. The magic of their bodies licked by flames and somehow still surviving lured me with its violence, the smoke-singe on their clothes, their hair, their skin.

At school, in the basement recreation room, with all the elementary grades, I'd sat cross-legged on the rust-orange rug while Jack Roach, the town's fire chief, paced in front of us in full firefighting gear, calling out questions like, "Why shouldn't you play with matches?" and "What should you do if you smell smoke?" He told us never touch a stove burner that's bright orange, don't ever put a can of gasoline beside a barbecue, and stop, drop, and roll if your clothes catch fire. Out of a paper grocery sack set on a table beside him, Chief

Roach pulled a hot dog wiener and stabbed it on the end of a long metal rod with a cord that dangled from its end.

"See this?" he said. "Looks harmless, doesn't it?" He plugged the pronged end of the cord into a small silver box the size of a toaster, then flicked a switch on the top of the box. Sparks shot from the wiener with a *pop*, followed by a fizzle and puff of smoke. The room lit up with shrieks and gasps. As the smoke haze cleared, flecks of char floated onto the table. All that was left of the wiener was a flayed chunk of blackened, sizzled meat.

Then, with the lights turned out and the projector whirring, we watched a film reel that told the story of one family's house fire. Sirens and red flashing lights, a ladder truck with hoses spraying into a billow of black smoke, men with axes smashing windows—it all seemed like an episode of an evening TV show, until the scene shifted to a hospital room where a girl, smaller than me, sat in a white gown on a table. From the knees down, her legs were red and blistered, and she was crying, the kind of crying that comes in jagged gasps, her open mouth a dark oblong howl. A nurse held a silver basin into which she dipped the girl's feet, slowly and one at a time, and then began to sponge water over the bright, burned legs. A close-up shot showed the girl's skin falling away like bits of tissue paper, slipping into the basin cloudy with her blood.

When the lights flicked back on, Chief Roach said, "And that's why you never play with fire."

I'd sat quiet in my row with the rest of my schoolmates but wanted to raise my hand and ask about the girl, what happened to her legs, and had they sewn the skin back on, bandaged it up like Lazarus from the Bible, dead three days before Jesus called for him to come forth out of his tomb and he stumbled back to life again.

Beside my grandparents' hearth, as Uncle Glen flexed the stub of his half-finger for the amazement of my cousins and me, I traced my own scars, thin white striations on my forehead and above my left eye, proof of the pain that once was, and before the scars, the blood.

"OKAY," CALLED GRANDMA. "We're ready to go."

She flicked the switch on the projector and it whirred into motion, throwing light onto the white screen set up at the far end of the living room.

She held up the film canister and read aloud the handwritten title on its label: *Barbecue, baptism*.

The first image stuttered into focus. The deep green of a summer lawn. A baby—Justin?—crying, and Aunt Lavonne scooping him up, kissing him on the cheek, turning away from us all in jittery Super-8 time, but in present tense on the chesterfield, laughing at her younger self, letting the room laugh with her.

Spliced together, fleet footage of a wheelbarrow race, a three-legged race, a potato-sack race, kids falling face-first into the lawn, rising grass-stained and stunned. Me in a blue sundress running barefoot with my cousins. Then bowls of potato salad on a picnic table. Hunks of meat—drumsticks, steaks—sizzling on a grill, smoke rising from the charcoal briquettes, and a man's hand with metal tongs entering the frame.

In the room's faltering dark, the story shifted to a tawny deer in the box of a white pickup, then blurred and zoomed in to its head hoisted by the antlers. On the tailgate, beside the buck, a baby sat clapping, smiling back at us.

"That's me!" Daniel hollered. "That's me!"

Then birch trees, and a river flowing. Four men in white shirts standing up to their waists in the current, lowering a young woman from the church's College and Careers group into the water, her long brown hair fanning out behind her as she floated back to air, smiling, wiping her eyes at the weight of this ritual, this imitating of the death of Jesus—gone down into the grave and then rising into life, that blood-soaked story at the centre of all our stories.

When the reel fluttered to its end and an empty screen, we kids rushed to be the stars, making ourselves shadows on white. With our hands outstretched, long fingers flexing, our silhouettes swayed in the brightness until Grandma flicked off the projector, leaving only the firelight. The darkened room settled back to quiet talk, the kind that lets the stories rise— first in quip and insult, one aunt taunting another, my mother saying, "No way, that's not what happened." Then Uncle John chiming in with his two cents and a fact recalled, a remember-when, like the time Uncle Glen chucked clods of dried horse manure through the outhouse window and hit Aunt Millie *conk* on the skull, and how Grandpa courted Grandma with after-church buggy rides, and that time he shot a moose at Shadow Lake—well, *in* Shadow Lake—and the beast dropped right there in the waist-high water, and Grandma had to wade out in her dress to help hoist that moose, drag it into the shallows where they could get a start on gutting it, this animal soaked through and pure dead weight.

At the end of one story and before the next began, a few moments of silence made space for a hush of meditation, like the pause of an amen after the prayer. But then another voice began, tentative, sounding its way into another story, telling of how the boys got hold of Aunt Lavonne's favourite doll—the one that cried when you tipped it backward—and sawed into its chest with a hunting knife to steal the voice box, and the one about catching crawdads and bullfrogs in the pond, and the frog legs they fried over a small flame on shore and ate straight off the whittled willow spear.

All our best stories had blood, and in that blood were more stories.

"Tell us another one, Uncle Glen," said a cousin—yes, tell us, said the others, and I jumped in with them, my voice eager in the chorus—another story, yes, the one about the grizzly and her cubs, the one where you had to shimmy up the tree and she almost clawed you down and sank her teeth into your neck, the time you almost died but lived to tell—tell us that one.

This Little Light

◇◇◇

SUMMER. IN OUR northern interior, it flicked on like a heat lamp. June's sudden shot of sun jolted everything green, from chickweed to poplars to the garden's seedling rows. At the tilt into July, bees hummed at every flower, and in the acres at the back of the property, among fireweed and thistle, wild strawberries reddened on their stems. With my brother and the neighbourhood kids, I ran barefoot through the rise and fall of the sprinkler's prismed arc. Some days, we carved out roads and tunnels for our Hot Wheels cars, each of us commanding a corner of the communal sandbox. Other days, we ripped around on our mini motorbikes, throttling down trails, pretending we were the Dukes of Hazzard County on the run from Boss Hogg and his sidekick, Rosco P. Coltrane.

By the middle of July, the novelty of time without structure had begun to wear off. With no early-morning wake-up, no running to catch the bus, no homework, no after-school piano lessons, each day blurred into the next until it seemed that all I did was sit inside the long, hot hours, sunburned and sweating, plucking the dry, prickly grass and shrieking away the wasps, waiting for something to break through the sameness.

Then, right at the threshold of August's monotony, it did.

"WHO'S EXCITED TO be here at VBS?" said Mrs. Penner from the church podium, smiling and cupping her hand to her ear. "I can't hear you, children!"

Me, me, me, we hollered back. I scooted to the edge of the pew full of girls my age and raised my hand high, a keener in the house of God.

VBS was Vacation Bible School, a free week-long program of games, arts and crafts, puppet shows, snacks, and Bible lessons run by our Evangelical Mennonite Church. Monday through Friday, morning until noon, I joined the horde of summer-bored kids eager to run through the sanctuary with a liberty never allowed during church services. Some of us were Sunday school kids, accustomed to the liturgy of songs and stories and the quiet, no-fidgeting-please-and-hands-to-yourselves prayer time that inevitably came at the close of every activity. Others were kids from the neighbourhood who had wandered over to the church to see what all the ruckus was about, then stuck around to drink the Kool-Aid and eat the free cookies.

"It's time to sing and praise the Lord," Mrs. Penner said, and clapped her hands to make us look her way. No matter the hellion back-row boys who chicken-farted and doled out Charley horses, Mrs. Penner smiled on, permed and twinkle-eyed and powdery with kindness.

Cousin Betty on accordion started up the opening notes, along with Aunt Mary on the vibraphone. Their tinny squeeze-box wheeze and smooth, velvety bells cast our song with an eerie cheer, like a sort of rising circus music.

Most of the words we sang, I didn't understand, but still they took me elsewhere. When we bellowed *Do Lord, oh do Lord, oh do remember me, way beyond the blue*, I eyed the bright velour fabric draped like a skirt around the vibraphone, sure that its royal-blue colour held a clue about the song's meaning. Aunt Mary with her mallets hit the keys to make a quivering *doooo* sound, a cool tremble that made me wonder if, way beyond the velvet blue, the Lord might recognize me, even know my name.

When we sang "If I Were a Butterfly," I saw myself in pinks and purples, a winged thing fluttering above a field of cartoon flowers. And when we sang about all the critters in creation having a place in God's choir, I became a bird on a taut tele-phone wire buzzing with voices, a chickadee in full song. I sang until I was another of the garden's wild creatures lifting off into the voltage of the sky, and no longer me down here, pale and stocky in my elastic-waisted rugby pants and smock blouse with the scratchy lace around the collar reddening my neck.

Around me, other children clapped along to the raucous song and fairly shouted, *This little light of mine, I'm gonna let it shine.* Though none of us had any idea what a bushel was, and why we wouldn't dare hide a little light under it, we all sang together as if we meant every word. I held my pointer finger up like a flaming candlewick. *Hide it under a bushel—* *no!* I belted out, assuming the words had something to do with the story of Moses and the desert bush on fire, and God's voice burning through to send him back to Egypt.

Later, after prayer and an amen dismissal, we stampeded down the stairs to the church basement, where a lineup of leaders stood waiting with clipboards in hand. Above the chatter of girls and the noise of boys locked in impromptu wrestling matches on the carpet, they called out names: *Wendy? Geneva? Steven K.? Steven D.?* Shushed into order and split into smaller groups, we shuffled off for the part of VBS that felt less like Vacation and more like School.

In a curtained-off corner, I sat with my fellow Juniors around a low U-shaped table, listening to Mr. Lonnie. He was younger than most of the leaders, a volunteer from the College and Careers group. His black, wavy hair was combed neatly to one side and slicked down to a shine, like a man in a shampoo commercial. As he talked, he flipped the pages of his fat lesson book and held it up for us to see the colour illustrations. Always, in every picture, Jesus stood at the centre of the story. Stretching out his hand toward a sick girl. Healing the lepers. Feeding the multitudes with a boy's loaves and fishes. Casting out a wild man's demons and sending them into a herd of pigs.

I'd heard it all before, in bedtime stories read aloud by my mother, in Sunday-school classrooms since I was old enough to talk. Jesus born in a manger. Jesus of Nazareth. Jesus the carpenter's son. Jesus in the temple, on the shore, in the boat, walking on the water. Jesus in the desert, in the garden, in the tomb, in the clouds, always kind-eyed, always wearing the same blue-and-white robe.

Every time I closed a prayer *in Jesus's name*, I felt the same quiet pride as when I plinked my quarter in the offering cup. In the mouths of soft-voiced women—my mother, my grandmothers, the women in the church—*Jesus* carried a lullaby's calm. From the tongues of men, it flashed like a double-edged sword. But I heard it spat, too, around the woodstove card games in my dad's shop, *Jesus* as a bitter hiss, a fed-up cuss to punctuate defeat. His name wasn't like other names. When I said it aloud—*Jesus*—I tasted a little of its hush and honey, and the sword and spark of it, too. Yet Jesus was, to me, like someone else's teddy bear—comforting in theory, but not close enough to be mine.

"Jesus loves you sooooo much," said Mr. Lonnie. "So much that he died on a cross for you." He stretched his hairy arms wide to show how much love, and to make a cross beam, like the one where Jesus hung. *Nails pounded in his hands*, he told us, and held his own thick-fingered hands up, palms toward us, *and nails in his feet, too*. I flashed back to my mother, weeks earlier, sprawled in the garden dirt with one shoe off, her mouth a tight circle of pain as she pulled a rusty nail from her heel.

I'd stepped barefoot on thistles, pricked my finger on a wild rose bush, snagged my skin on the barbed-wire fence, but the crown of thorns set down on Jesus's head—thorns like thumbtacks, like the sharpened points of screws—that cruelty made my throat cinch tight. I knew the story well, had seen it pantomimed in Sunday-school Easter plays with a flimsy lumber cross dragged up the aisle and a papier-mâché stone rolled away from a cardboard tomb. But that morning in the church basement, as I listened to Mr. Lonnie tell us again about the bag of silver and Judas's kiss, the purple robe and crown of thorns, the Roman soldier hammering in the nails, the old story sounded different. It made my stomach feel weird, partly because as Mr. Lonnie told it, his words wheezed out of him, as if he'd swallowed the squeaker from a waterlogged dog toy, or was trying hard not to sob.

"Can you believe it?" he said. "Can you believe that Jesus died for me? For you?" He held open the lesson book to a picture of Jesus hanging, chin to his chest, slumped and bleeding on the cross and naked, except for what looked like a bunched-up cloth diaper about to slip off his limp body. Even the noisy boys stayed quiet, leaning in toward the violence as we studied the illustration.

After he set down the book, Mr. Lonnie pulled from his bag of lesson supplies a rubber-banded stack of glossy red pamphlets and began to hand them out. They looked like brochures, the kind displayed at the medical clinic, advertising help for infections and diseases. *Three Steps to Knowing Jesus*, proclaimed the cover.

It was a tract, Mr. Lonnie told us, and we could follow the steps inside the tract, on our own, alone in a quiet spot, and Jesus would hear us if we talked to Him, as if we were the only ones praying. "Whenever someone invites Jesus to come in," said Mr. Lonnie, "the angels in heaven celebrate."

I thought about it as I stood in line to receive my oatmeal cookie and cup of purple juice. I thought about it as I stood at the craft station gluing popsicle sticks into a frame that held a Polaroid of my face and below it, in sparkle-glitter letters, my name. I thought about it as we held hands and trudged in a circle in the parking lot behind the church, singing *the farmer picks a wife*, and *the wife picks a child*, and the child a nurse, the nurse a cow, all the way down the line of "The Farmer in the Dell" until Clarence Harder, the cheese, stood alone, sweating in the sun. My mind was elsewhere, still on the cross. If Jesus loved me enough to wear those thorns and let the blood run down into his long brown hair, the least I could do was ask him to come into my heart. A tiny house painted red with a brick chimney puffing smoke—that's how I imagined it, and Jesus standing outside the little door, patient as an old dog, waiting for me to open the door and let him come inside.

I MADE SURE my bedroom door was locked, that I would be alone. I pulled the curtains shut and clicked on my bedside lamp. Its glow threw a lace-edged circle of light over my feet. I liked the feeling of standing in it, and how the room grew serious around me, my skin prickling in the quiet. I unfolded the glossy tract and spread it open on my bed. Three cartoon numbers stared up at me with goggle eyes. In a white speech bubble, a smiling number one decreed: *Admit that you're a sinner, and that you've made mistakes.*

I knelt on the carpet, clasped my hands, bowed my head, and closed my eyes.

"Dear Jesus," I whispered, following the words prescribed to me for everlasting life.

Like the spool of music on Grandpa and Grandma Funk's player piano cranked by some hidden ghost hand, sins rolled up through my mind. My fat mitten slapped across Dustin's red cheek. The snapped antenna from the radio-pack of my brother's Six Million Dollar Man. My crayon scribbles and ripped pages in the colouring book, above which I'd forged my younger cousin's name. *Look, Mom,* I'd said, *she's wrecking everything.* Once begun, the reel of trespasses played on. The orange-haired baby's neck fat pinched so I could hear him cry. The lemon drop stolen from the belly of the blue glass hen when my mother wasn't looking. And the daddy longlegs spider I trapped inside an empty pickle jar, watching as it tried to scrabble up the glass. I tipped it onto the carport floor and, one by one, plucked off its legs until a single threadlike leg remained, then watched it drag in circles on the concrete.

"I am a sinner," I whispered. "I have made mistakes."

The tract's cartoon 2 with its wide-open mouth speech-bubbled the second step: Believe that Jesus died for you and rose again, and ask him to forgive your sins.

I knew Jesus had died, like Mr. Lonnie told us, but for me, I wasn't sure. I couldn't figure out how back in Bible-times Jerusalem he knew what I'd do wrong here, in Vanderhoof, all these years and miles away from where he walked the earth. But if alive and spying down from Heaven's lofty vantage, then of course he saw it all, even me. And if he could see every sin and secret, of course he had to have risen from the grave. How else to explain his all-knowingness, his everywhere-ness. The riddle of that logic rolled back and forth in my mind, a stone unsealing and sealing up the tomb.

In Sunday-morning worship, the female voices, silver and flutey, together sang the question, *What can wash away my sins?* And the men sang back in a deep, mahogany drone, *Nothing but the blood of Jesus.* I thought of the bloodstains on the knees of my baby-blue corduroy pants when I wiped out on my bike. The blood crusted in my hair, oozing from my split lip, road rash on my chin and cheeks when I fell down, down, down. How blood could cancel any stain, erase sin's black X and leave a clean white space, only made sense by miracle, the kind Jesus performed when he waved his hand over jars of water and changed them into wine. What holy magic he wielded, how one word from his mouth made the storm go still and the waves go slack, remained mysterious. But not every mystery needed to be solved for the story to be true. All I had to do was look at stars pinpricked into darkness. Even without me knowing why and how, they shone.

I meant it when I said the words—*Please forgive my sins*—and let them all be washed away, the way the stuck-on smears of dead insects disappeared as the windshield wipers waved back and forth over the glass and made clear the road ahead. And when I spoke the tract's third and final step that assured an eternity with God—*Confess with your mouth that Jesus is Lord*—I felt the warmth spill over me, like when I lay back in the bathtub to let my mother wash my hair, the water scooped with a plastic cup and poured over my head, the heat trickling back from my forehead, down around my ears and neck so that my whole body shivered. Those words I spoke aloud—like a charm to change a creature into something new—charged the room, hung in the quiet around me, every syllable aglow.

Elsewhere in the house, my brother raked through Lego, building another fighter jet, battle-ready. Below me, in the basement laundry room, the ironing board creaked open to receive the clothesline's load, and my mother smoothed out the wrinkles. Down the Kluskus logging road, my dad gripped the truck's steering wheel, craning through a cloud of summer dust. But in the solitude of my pink-walled bedroom, even before I opened my eyes and unclasped my hands, I felt it—the beginning and the shift. I was like a birthday girl, floating to the centre of the story, clean and pressed and ready for the party, for the stack of wrapped and curly-ribboned gifts, for the cake blazing with candles and a cluster of guests leaning in, waiting for me to take a breath and blow.

When someone asks Jesus into their heart, Mr. Lonnie said, all of Heaven celebrates. From the beige shag rug in the middle of my room where I knelt, I tried to see past the stippled ceiling flecked with silver sparkles and picture the scene—high above the roofline, through the clouds, angels flexing their wings, swooping along the streets of gold, circling the sea of glass and a huge, smoke-wreathed throne, blasting brassy trumpets as they flew.

All that the verses and sermons proclaimed on long and boring Sundays—*You are the salt of the earth, a city on a hill, a vessel of clay out of whose cracks spill treasure*—had always sounded like words to a song meant for someone else to sing, promises made to the robed and bearded Bible men who followed Jesus around like a pack of hungry strays. But

Jesus—the one Mr. Lonnie called "Light of the World"—he seemed to have climbed down an invisible ladder, away from Heaven's revelry, to stand outside my heart and knock and knock and knock until I finally let him in. I stood in the centre of my bedroom, wearing the same clothes, but feeling like something had finally happened, like I'd changed. *Do, Lord, oh, do Lord.* I clicked off my bedside lamp and unlocked my door. *Hide it under a bushel, no!* In my gut, an ember, as if I'd swallowed all the candles off the birthday cake, and my face flush with the heat. I stepped over the threshold into the cool shadows of the hallway on whose walls hung photos of the girl I used to be.

The Horse
Story

◇◇◇

LIKE A PARABLE, my grandfather's story of the horse burned
with a wisdom beyond the earthly. Every detail seemed
to catch the mind's eye with a shimmer that said, *Look*,
that said, *Listen*. The river, sluggish and low that summer, but
still flowing. The sun's high-vaulted heat simmering the elements, tipping the odds out of his favour. The buzz of insects
at his sweaty head, and the smell—that off, sweet rot cooking
around him. Though he didn't remember the horse's name—
Cricket? Smoky? Or maybe Methuselah?—he could call up that
day of his boyhood without effort, rebuilding that long-ago
world for the listener, and taking me back to the farm on the
outskirts of an Oregon town called Sweet Home.

It was the first time his father had left him in charge of
the property. His parents needed to make a trip into town, a

full day's journey there and back, and his older sister, Mildred, would go along, but he, the only son, needed to stay behind. Though only twelve, he was old enough now to look after the livestock and to take on the daily rhythm of chores. He watched his family, dressed in their Sunday clothes, ride away in the buggy drawn by two bay horses, and felt a swell of pride at the burden of this day. His father, a man in whose shadow he gladly walked, whose footsteps in the dirt he followed, trusted him. A light fear threatened to creep in, but rather than mull the what-ifs that whirred on the fringes of his thinking—what if a stranger, what if a storm—he set to work.

As soon as he reached the barn, he knew something was wrong. The old plough horse was listless, leaning against the stall. When he scattered in a handful of oats, the creature didn't eat. Not even a flicker of the ears. Within an hour of him being left in charge, the horse lay down in the stall's far corner and refused to lift its head from the hay. He tried to rouse it, thinking colic, a twisted gut, and finally prodded the animal to its feet. He pulled it by the halter out into the paddock. The horse, breathing hard, stumbled, faltered. And then it was done. The horse stiffened where it stood, shuddered, and then crumpled over in the stink of its own manure.

To everything there is a season—a time to live, a time to die—and that late morning brought the horse's death rattle to the farm. He'd seen animals killed by a quick snap of the neck, with an axe, a rifle. He'd knelt beside his father in the woods and pulled the innards from a buck, but never up close and in real time had he witnessed the natural end of a creature. The horse's breath leaked out, like air from a slashed tire, and left the cheeks hollow, the rib cage gaunt.

The problem he faced now was what to do with the body. Not even noon, and the sun threw a heat warp over the field. He stalked across the yard to check the henhouse's wire fence for holes, pumped fresh water for the troughs. He stacked what lumber needed stacking. He surveyed the acres—the barn, the house, the dirt road—found them all quiet, unnervingly so, but in good order. He thought of where his folks and sister might be now. His mother standing at a store counter, studying her list of goods. His sister at their mother's side, a slim shadow in a white bonnet. His father talking with other men from the church about the price of wheat and wood, and who needed work, and whose crops this season suffered grasshoppers. He felt certain that this day was a test, and that his father, upon returning home, would judge how well he'd fared.

By early afternoon, the horse had begun to bloat. Under the high sun, its belly swelled like a broodmare due to birth twin foals. The stench, too, was rising: a sick and sweet perfume hung in the air. When a breeze tilted across the barnyard, it carried the odour toward him. Once he smelled it, he couldn't shake it, the vapour trail haunting him, as if the horse were breathing at his back, pressing him to fix the wrong that festered.

He tried to drag the thing by its back legs, but even with all his weight anchored and leaning, the most he could do was shift its shape in the dirt. Each tug and yank only wafted the stench toward him. Sweat-drenched, gut muscles clenched, he pulled. Pulled hard. But no use. Flies congregated on the horse's rusty coat, black spots rising, hovering, settling to feed.

He squatted in the shade of the barn's lean-to and thought: what would his father do?

And here, Grandpa let his listener offer up ideas, thoughts of how best he should tackle the problem, guesses on what he should do with that horse. Stick a blade in the belly to let out the pent-up gases? Butcher it right there in the muck of the paddock? Leave the creature be until his father came home to help?

He knew the tractor key hung on a nail in the tool shed. His father didn't like him driving it without permission, but he weighed the circumstances. Seeing as how he was the one in charge of the farm, taking his father's place, he might be the one to give himself permission. He slipped the key from its nail, grabbed a shovel, coiled two chains over his shoulder, and headed for the tractor.

After swinging open the gate and backing the tractor into the paddock, as close to the horse as he could get without running over a hoof, he set to work with the chains. He wrestled them beneath the horse's shoulder, then looped them around and behind the front legs, making sure they hooked around the girth where the joints met the belly. It took him a few tries and tugs to fit the chains so that the thousand pounds of horse would budge, and finally, when he let out the clutch and eased the gas, the tractor lurched, and the dead weight moved. Out of the swung-open paddock gate he drove, the engine straining and a cloud of exhaust fumes blooming up, the cargo behind leaving a flattened, smooth swath of earth in its wake.

He hauled it to the field nearest the river. Slack in its chains, the horse lay stiff-legged, locked in position but still swelling. He'd been worried the beast might burst while being pulled, but miracle of miracles, the belly held.

As he dug the blade into the earth, he guessed how many shovelfuls remained. Three hundred. Two hundred. No, five hundred more. The hole, he knew, needed to be bigger than the horse, but still, he hadn't known the long hours this digging would take. Without a tree to shade him, he felt as though the sun were cooking him alive. His hands fattened with heat, and his feet tightened in his boots. His pulse throbbed in his head, sun-hammered, dizzy. He stopped only to wipe sweat from his eyes or take a swig of water from the jug.

By the time the hole was deep enough to hold the body, the sun had begun to cast an amber dazzle over the river. The horse, dragged the final distance, slid rigid into the earth. Then he noticed the problem. Though the back legs were bent tight and close to the body, one of the forelegs—the left—locked at the knee, stuck straight up. With the horse lying on its back in the hole, the stiffened limb jutted above ground level. When he stood a few paces back, the hoof and fetlock were still visible. He tried to work the leg down, but no use. With rigor mortis having settled, it was like trying to bend a block of wood.

Because he wanted to finish the job and have his father, upon returning, see the paddock horseless, ask to hear the story, then say to him, *Well done, son*, he shovelled the mound of loamy dirt back into the hole. Dust to dust, he thought, like any old gravedigger. Each shovelful erased the horse a little more until the neck and withers disappeared, then the eerie half-shut eye, the black mane, and finally the rusty, bloated belly. What remained, though, was that foot, stuck like a blunt question mark above the plot.

Here, again, Grandpa's eyes crinkled, his face still solemn with the telling, but he let the listener lean in, surprised, maybe let out a little laughter to accompany the curiosity and comedy. A horse's hoof! He paused long enough to let on that this was still a wisdom story, the kind that brought a lesson along with it, and if we pressed in further, the truth would come clear. For the big illumination, I hadn't the language yet, but even without being able to say *metaphor* and *symbol*, I knew a story's power to carry my mind elsewhere and to other thoughts. That hoof poking out of the ground and my grandpa's boyhood shoveling made me think of other deaths I knew, other plots of dirt. Aunt Linda in her pale-blue dress descending. My cousin beneath the closed lid of that sinking coffin. The uncle buried beneath a tombstone in an Oregon churchyard—Uncle Howard, the ghost baby no one spoke of anymore. He would have been the eldest, my grandmother once said, but he came too early. A blue-skinned stillborn too small to live.

He drove the tractor up the slope and into the lean-to, hung the key in the tool shed, and grabbed a hacksaw, then headed back down to the field. With the shovel, he dug down around the foot, clearing enough room to finish the work. Then, in the same way he'd fit the blade to a notch in a tree trunk, he pulled that saw into place at the knee joint. He let the teeth catch, then snag into the flesh and tendon. He pulled the hacksaw back and forth, slowly, until it found the bone, then kept the blade moving. A little blood oozed. Flies droned around his face. And that bone, with his final passes of the saw, splintered. He cracked it off and nicked away the skin left clinging until the hoof came free in his hand.

Had he stood there with his eyes closed a moment, the heft of that horse's foot in his grip could have been a mossy length of punky alder, solid, but hollow, too, the hoof unshod, striated with cracks from two decades of trod miles, frost and snow, mud and dust, man's work and beast's work. I held that foot, too, in my mind's eye, and saw my grandfather—that serious boy in the black-and-white photograph resting on the mantle—standing still in the field, wondering what came next.

He carried it down toward the shore. On the weedy bluff, with the water twisting and whorling below, he cocked his arm back, then pitched the foot, that bloodless stump floating a moment at the peak of its arc—a flying thing held above the sun, as if free and with a will to choose height or depth, rise or fall, light or dark—then pitching down into the river. A splash, white froth, and the rusty stump bobbing to the surface as the current took it south toward the sea.

In the silence that followed Grandpa's story, a smile threatened to break over his face, but he always held back, letting the listener sit with the question of what it all meant. What happened when his folks came home, what his father said about the dead horse, all that shoveling, the sawed-off foot—he never told. He hooked his thumbs in his belt loops, tilted his head a little to the side, and clicked his tongue against his teeth like punctuation, an ellipsis that left the story open and inscribed in me a question mark.

The hot sun, the boy alone and in his father's place, the horse's body bloating in the heat—I heard them like the elements of a Sunday sermon or a story from an ancient text. I knew they meant more than the sum of their parts. A boy working his father's farm sounded like scripture, like a missive from a far-off kingdom. Death beneath the sun conjured Christ sweating in the desert, the body breaking down, aching toward the final Resurrection. My grandfather, the boy, staring into that hole in the earth, mulling his own end.

I imagined that horse's foot travelling down the river, and the dead-uncle ghost baby floating, too, joining with the horse's hoof, hooked together in a chain, like a starter strand of DNA, cast out but swimming toward the rivers of eternity, where one day we all will meet. And there, Grandpa will tell the story all over again, patting that horse on the shoulder as it shakes off the flies and sweat, and the stillborn will be no longer blue at the lips but spark-eyed and standing near in the field—a boy, a horse, a man, all held inside the bigger story, the one we all were made for, and are forever carried toward.

Every Hidden Thing

◇◇◇

B E SURE YOUR *sins will find you out.* The iambic pulse of my mother's words sounded like a warning spoken in a fairy tale, a glowing bony finger pointed at my heart, the final sentence of a Sunday-school lesson in which the story ends in fire or flood or famine. When she recited this proverb, she tilted her head a little to the side and raised one eyebrow, and spoke in the same dark tone she used when a pickup had run over our cocker spaniel: *She should have listened when I called.*

We lived in a surveillance state. Though Jesus had long gone back to Heaven, rocketing up post-Resurrection, light shooting from the holes in his hands, he'd left behind the Holy Ghost, who could be anywhere, and was, and all the time kept

watching like my mother. When alone in my parents' bedroom I picked up my dad's coin bank, a ceramic monk with a
fluffy tonsure and a painted-on sad face, and fiddled with the
rubber plug that stopped the dimes and quarters from spilling
into my palm, I sensed the eyes behind me: the Holy Ghost or
Mom—I couldn't tell. When I cracked open the refrigerator in
my dad's shop to the brown bottles on the shelves and thought
of the cold, bitter Pilsner on my tongue, the whisper in my ear
intoned with a haunting quaver: *Be sure . . . be sure . . . be sure
your sins will find you out.*

That summer morning when the telephone rang and
Grandpa Shenk told my mother to hurry up, get in the pickup
and meet him back at their house, but come right away, she
thought something was seriously wrong. Grandpa wouldn't
tell her over the phone why she needed to come, only that he
needed her *right away, right now, just come.* So we climbed
into our mint-green Chrysler and gunned it up the hill and
through the asphalt's heat-shimmer toward Grandma and
Grandpa's house. When we pulled into their driveway, other
cars and trucks were waiting. Uncle Wayne stood sweating
at the back of his pickup's open box, pulling a stack of pallets
to the edge of the tailgate, motioning for us to come and take
our pick.

Grandpa lived a secret life that only the family knew about.
On his visits to the town dump, under the guise of dropping
off his own garbage, tossing a black plastic bag onto the smoking heap, he waited until he was sure no one was watching
him, and then he'd sneak, cap pulled down to shield his face,
and begin scouring for free junk, anything worth plucking

from the pile. A lamp without its shade. A broom without its bristles. A stack of Hardy Boys with the pages only slightly waterlogged, only faintly smelling of cat pee. At family gatherings, he quietly displayed his latest finds, pulling us aside to show how he'd cleaned up the thing, repaired it, made it almost good as new.

"Can you believe someone actually threw this away?" he'd say, holding up an axe with a splintered handle or a bent can opener or a telephone missing its coiled cord.

Their toy box overflowed with scavenged things. Rusty Tonka trucks and die-cast metal cars, teddy bears restitched, restuffed, wooden blocks that needed sanding and repainting, a smudge-faced doll with an eye that never fully closed or a head of hair left too close to the heater and now melted to a matted plastic clump.

That morning, Grandpa had arrived at the dump to see the Dairyland truck backed up to one of the junk heaps. The uniformed driver stood at the back of the truck, the doors swung open, unloading pallets of ice cream.

"Past its best before," said the driver, nodding to my grandpa. "Shame to see it go to waste."

Grandpa poked around the dump, fiddled with the junk in the back of his pickup, and waited for the driver to finish unloading. As soon as the dairy truck drove out of sight, he began hefting the pallets into the back of his truck. When he realized that his truck wasn't roomy enough to carry all the ice cream, he drove to a payphone and called my uncle for backup. The two of them worked like bandits on the lam, hurrying to load the ice cream before it melted in the sun and before anyone else pulled into the yard, then speeding down the dump road with a dust cloud in their wake and hundreds of cartons in their trucks.

Once back at my grandparents' house, they began calling the rest of the family.

"Hurry up," Grandpa said. "It won't stay frozen long."

By the time we arrived, other aunts and uncles and cousins filled the yard, everyone gathered around the back of Grandpa's pickup, pointing, exclaiming "Black Cherry!" and "Tiger Tail" and "a whole pallet of Chocolate Chip Mint!" At a time when gallon buckets of Neapolitan were our household norm, this array of flavours was our own manna in the wilderness.

Each family claimed a share of the cartons, which had begun to sweat and drip in the heat. Because "best before" dates and the fact that most folks didn't get groceries at the dump were beyond me, I failed to pay full attention to my mother and her siblings huddled around Grandpa, holding an impromptu family meeting in which low voices uttered phrases like "don't say anything" and "our good name" and "what would people think?"

LATER, THAT EVENING, before Janice, the neighbour girl, arrived to look after us while my parents went to an Elks Hall dinner and dance, my mother sat me and my brother down on the living room sofa. She leaned in toward us with the look of one about to foretell a plague of locusts, her eyes the serious, scary kind.

"You will not," she said, "tell Janice about the ice cream. Do you understand?"

My brother bounced on the edge of his couch cushion. "About how Grandpa stole it from the dump?"

"Grandpa did not steal it," my mother said. "Dairyland threw it away. And anyways, it's fine to eat. And there's nothing wrong with it. And it was free. We didn't steal it." Her words came fast, spilled out.

She made us promise and repeat after her: not one word about the ice cream. Yes, if we finished our supper, we could eat some for dessert. Yes, one bowl each. Yes, three scoops, okay, four scoops if we're good. But not one word about the ice cream. Not a single word.

Had my mother said nothing about the ice cream, had she not made us promise, I would have licked my bowl clean and simply asked for more. But her intensity, and the hard glint in her eyes when she made me repeat back to her the pledge that I would keep the secret, made the secret glitter illicitly. I was too young to consider what others might think of us eating food retrieved from the town dump. I had no reputation to uphold. I only had the ice cream, and the secret inside me that grew and thrummed as the evening wound down toward bedtime.

"Our mom said we can have ice cream before bed," my brother said. He shot me a look, nervous, on edge. "It's really good ice cream. You can have some, too. It's really good to eat." His voice was more eager and higher-pitched than normal.

Janice, whose heavy-lidded eyes made her seem perpetually drowsy, whose nose was so big I couldn't help but stare at it, stood with us over the panorama of cartons as we chose. "That's a whole lot of ice cream," she said.

"We *really* love ice cream," I said. "Even when it comes from—" my brother elbowed me in the ribs.

Janice let us scoop our three scoops and filled her own bowl high. We sat in the living room, Janice on the chair, my brother and me on the sofa, swapping looks between spoonfuls. Before I even spoke the truth aloud, I felt it on my tongue, as if the very letters were practicing formation for their arrival into syllable and sound. The questions formed, too, like why did my mother want to keep it hidden, and what was the big deal about free ice cream, and did other people get ice cream from the dump, and didn't the ice cream mean we'd won the prize? Janice, smiling at me over her bowl of rainbow sherbet, spooned into her mouth what I already knew. My mother's warning hummed from far away, but too far off to haunt.

"I bet you'll never guess where we got this ice cream from," I said. At the thrill of this edge, teetering from secret to full-out revelation, my heart hammered in my throat.

"Hmmm," she said. "Maybe the Co-op?"

"Nope."

My brother jabbed the handle of his spoon into my leg and glowered at me.

"Shoppers Food Mart?" Janice tried again.

"Wrong," I said.

"Lucky Dollar?"

Again I shook my head. She was running out of grocery stores.

"Don't," my brother seethed through gritted teeth. "Don't you tell." He stood up and stared down at me where I sat cross-legged in my pajamas, wide-smiling at the dam about to burst.

"The dump!" I blurted. "We got this ice cream from the dump!"

Janice cocked her head. "The dump?" Her smile straightened, then slipped. "Actually the dump?"

I felt a swell of triumph. I'd said the thing I wasn't supposed to say, and it felt like victory, the same surge of heat that came with being right, scoring highest, having my name called aloud in Sunday-school class for the monthly perfect attendance award.

My brother rushed to explain about Grandpa, how he liked to dig through garbage for stuff, how the truck driver said the ice cream was still okay to eat, it wasn't rotten or gross, that all our cousins had dump ice cream at their houses, too, plus it was free, free ice cream, all you can eat, like a smorgasbord— but free. What was left in her bowl, Janice didn't finish. She washed our empty dishes, quiet in the kitchen, cleaning up the mess we'd left behind, saying little.

"You weren't supposed to tell," my brother hissed as we headed down the hallway toward our bedrooms. I knew I'd trespassed our mother's words, but nothing I'd said was a lie. I had no frame of reference for the decorum of family secrets, hadn't yet learned that some information stayed behind the veil, because *what would people think*. I had barely begun noticing that before we drove to church or to a gathering on her side of the family, my mother always made a quick clean sweep of the pickup. She took the bottle of rye whisky tucked in its brown bag out of the side door and stuck it in the garage. She emptied the ashtray into the woodstove and hung a new pine-tree air freshener from the rearview mirror. She covered up what she felt needed covering. But to me, my dad's smoking habit, our cable TV channels, the Kenworth swimsuit calendar of half-naked ladies tacked on the shop wall—these were still only details from our ordinary world, not yet facts of life that needed hiding.

I WOKE TO my mother drawing open my curtains and letting in a sudden stream of sunlight so bright it made me squint. She sat down on the end of my bed, quiet. It was Sunday morning, and she had already dressed for church in a skirt and blouse, but her hair was still rolled in pink foam curlers. Across her lap, she held the wooden spoon.

"I told you not to tell." She tipped her chin down, which made her eyes dark and sad. "Not anyone."

We didn't want to be known as the family who scavenged for dessert amid smouldering tires and rusty old stoves, did we?

We didn't.

We didn't want to people to think of us as dirty, as dump-divers, did we?

Clearly, we did not.

When I bent over the bed and offered myself to the wooden spoon, squeezing out tears as was my usual trick to lighten the blows, the music of the proverb hit me again. *Be sure. Your sins. Will find. You out.* For every flavour tasted—Candy Cane with flecks of red-and-green crushed peppermint, Tiger Tail swirled orange and black, Tin Roof Sundae ribboned with fudge and roasted peanuts, and the rainbow swirl of sherbet melting on my tongue—one quick *thwack* of the wooden spoon on my pajamaed backside. With every *thwack*, my mother's words struck like revelation. She was right. The child who steals the honey from the comb, who breaks the oath, will be found out. Every hidden thing rises to the light. Every secret will be sussed, hoisted from the heap of junkyard shadows and held up as proof, that the one whose deeds are done in darkness will always be brought out into the open, laid bare for every eye to see.

The Lady of the Lake

◇◇◇

L ATE FRIDAY AFTERNOON, in the high heat of July, my dad rumbled down the driveway in his logging truck, his week of night shifts in the bush behind him, those long hours and miles of hauling logs over washboard gravel roads. He swung open the front door of the house and called up the stairs.

"Hurry up," he said, "get ready, we're going camping at the lake."

As my mother brisked from fridge to cupboard to cooler, packing our sudden rations and loading up for a weekend away, she clucked her tongue, sighed, and shook her head over my dad's decreed spontaneity, for which he had little responsibility except to hook up the trailer and drive.

For the early years of my childhood, our family camping happened inside an oiled canvas cabin tent so awkward and heavy it took all four of us—my dad and mom each hefting one end, and my brother and me with the wooden poles, ropes, and stakes—to carry it from the box of the pickup to the pitching site. But at the start of that summer, my dad drove into the yard towing a fifth-wheel trailer behind his pickup.

"A house on wheels," he said, and flung open the door, motioning for my mother to step inside for the grand tour. A narrow galley kitchen with a diner-style booth. A scratchy plaid hide-a-bed with sagging cushions. And up the four stairs carpeted in green shag rug, two narrow captain bunks with a nightstand between them. The colour scheme— rust and avocado—betrayed the second-hand trailer's early-seventies origins, but the bones of the RV were solid, my dad promised.

"What's wrong with the tent?" my mother said. "I like the tent."

But my dad insisted that this was a great deal, and besides, he'd already paid for it, cash, on the spot, no returns.

"It'll be our family getaway," he said. "Our home away from home."

IN THE BACK seat with my brother, I counted telephone poles, tried not to ask again how long until we got there. My mother glanced again and again in the rearview mirror, eyeing the fifth-wheel trailer that listed behind as if it might unhitch around the curve in the road. Up the Yellowhead Highway, past the reserve with its low-roofed, plywood-sided houses, over the bridge and down a gravel road flanked by fireweed and willows, we lurched.

Fraser Lake was just under an hour's drive from home, past the lumber mills, the truck weigh scales, and past Fort Fraser, the tiny village that was once a fur-trading post. We followed the railway and the river west, but as my dad steered us toward our weekend trip, I wasn't thinking about geography and history. I knew nothing of the ancient lava beds and the Red Rock volcano, of the thousand trumpeter swans that wintered on the Nautley River, or of the pictographs of the Indigenous tribes who first walked the territory. With my dad at the wheel, our family focus was fixed: drive fast to claim the biggest campsite. Windows rolled down, the local country station blaring classic hits, we headed into the glare of sun and billows of dust rising from a caravan of campers, trucks, and trailers heading for the lake.

We were escaping for a more spacious place, or at least, my dad's version of it, a place where the party hooted all day and roared all night. He was happiest at the centre of the noise and crowd, calling for another round of drinks, another log on the fire. In our camping crew of relatives and friends, my dad was among his own kind, never alone with his bottle of beer or cup of Crown Royal. At the lake, the Sunday church pew didn't haunt him. No logging truck's flat tire or monkey-wrenching called him away from his game of cards. He could sit by the fire however long he wanted to without my mother telling him he'd better go to bed. As soon as we turned off onto the narrow lane that zigzagged through the campground's fir and pines, he grew light and loose at the wheel, tapping the dash to the beat of the radio's song.

"Looks like the biggest one," said my dad, as he backed the fifth-wheel trailer into our spot.

The sites around filled with the usual crowd, the party growing in noise and bodies. Our camping clan was made up of my dad and three of his brothers—brothers who, like him, didn't feel enough guilt to sit through a sermon every Sunday. Along with their wives and kids, some fellow truckers and lumber-mill friends, and a small group of families who'd immigrated from what was then Yugoslavia, we formed our own lakeside tribe.

As eager as we'd been to leave behind the daily rhythms of home, camp life quickly fell into a parallel and familiar pattern. The boys, a pack of them with slingshots in their pockets, wandered the network of trails that wound through the trees. The men unloaded firewood from the backs of pickups and broke out cases of beer. The women set to work recreating a sense of domestic order, wiping off the picnic tables and laying out communal trays of cookies, potato chips, and thermoses of juice. My dad made his rounds, going from trailer to camper to motorhome door, shooting the breeze and offering to pour a free drink from his brown-bagged whisky bottle to anyone who was thirsty. And when he grew restless, he called our names, told my mother to put down her dishcloth, and motioned for us to follow him.

"Let's head down to the water," he said, "and go for a ride on *The Lady of the Lake*."

The Lady of the Lake belonged to his buddy Sparky. He'd spent years designing and crafting the forty-foot houseboat, and had used my dad's shop as his work space. When he finally launched it, our family had been there to watch him and his wife, Viola, a tall, brassy-haired Swedish woman, smash a bottle of Baby Duck champagne on one of the bright-red metal pontoons.

As we neared the water, we heard the unmistakable horn, a half-honk air raid siren that cut through the light wind and carried across the lake. *The Lady of the Lake* was far from elegant, and looked less like a sleek vessel than like a compact portable trailer bolted atop a barge. As the houseboat motored toward us, red and white and boxy, my dad grinned. He had never learned to swim, was fearful of the water, and yet, as soon as that boat motored toward shore, as soon as the bow gate swung open and the ramp lowered to welcome guests aboard, he grew light and loose, jokey and bright. I felt it, too—that thrill at being lifted out of the ordinary and set adrift into possibility.

When I stood on the open front deck, I felt like a child movie star, waving at beachgoers on shore, thinking *I am here, and you are there, I am going somewhere, and you are not*. To the strangers we passed, my dad pulled off his ball-cap and tipped it above his head like a captain's hello. Up and down the lake we cruised, with Sparky setting course and trading off with my dad at the wooden ship's wheel. In the cabin, my mother sat alongside Viola and the other wives.

With the sun angling down toward the horizon and gulls circling in the cirrus-streaked sky, the houseboat scraped to a stop on the shore of a small, nameless island at the east end of the lake. There, Sparky tossed out a rope and my dad looped it around a piece of driftwood. The men gathered driftwood and over it, my dad poured gasoline from a jerry can, then tossed a lit match to spark a fast, high blaze. When the flames settled, the adults dragged lawn chairs and blocks of wood into a circle around the fire, and we kids took off to explore.

Away from the fire, I took off my shoes and socks and rolled up my pant cuffs to wade in the shallows. With a Styrofoam cup, I tried to scoop minnows that darted around my ankles, but every step lifted a murky cloud of silt and made it hard to see. Farther out, the water rippled black and revved with the engines of evening speedboaters jetting in circles, going nowhere in the chop.

WHEN I WADED out of the water, little brown clots clustered around my ankles and dotted my calves. Specks of mud or lake-slime splotches, I thought, and bent over to brush them off. As my fingers slid over the slickness of what clung, what wouldn't come unstuck, what clearly wasn't mud, I knew the truth.

I kicked, but they didn't shake loose. I thrashed my arms and legs as I took off shrieking down the beach, but the leeches with their razor teeth held on. Before I could reach my mother and before Viola could grab a salt shaker from the houseboat galley kitchen, my dad stood up from his block of wood and with a fluid single movement, tucked his cigarette to the side of his mouth and grabbed my arm.

"Hold still a minute," he said. He reached into his left chest pocket, took out his lighter, and thumbed it to a tiny flame.

With one hand, despite my squirming, my dad anchored me, and with the other hand, he brought the lighter close enough for me to feel the heat on my leg. I feared the worst—

that I'd burn, too, like that girl in the fire safety film—but my dad held the lighter steady. At its singe, the first leech shrivelled, dropped to the rocks.

One by one, each leech shrank and fell away, leaving behind a thin trickle of red at its sucking site. My dad thumbed away the blood and wiped it on his pant leg, and when my legs were clean and free of leeches, he turned me loose, went back to his stump, and rejoined the circle.

WHEN WE BOARDED the houseboat for the trip back across the lake, when we reached the campground shore and trailed back to the site and the company of campers roasting marshmallows and pouring more drinks, when I climbed the four shag steps to the upper bunk and my narrow captain's bed with the old foam mattress, all I wanted was to go home. Across from me, my brother's bed lay empty. Somewhere in the trees, well away from the watchful eyes of parents, he huddled in his sleeping bag, murmuring in the boys' tent. All the day's heat and sun had drained away from the forest and the lake, leaving the night air with a chill that threatened frost. I slipped into my cold sleeping bag. Through the screen of the tiny sliding window, men's voices poured forth laughter, then fell to quiet, all of them listening to one man speak, until finally they roared back again with the joke's punchline, the story's next turn. All the while, the pull of an accordion droned through the talking, a low harmony that swung into a slow *oompah-pah*.

At home, every night as I lay beneath a hand-stitched patchwork comforter, my mother's face would hover as she joined me in saying our bedtime prayer—*Now I lay me down to sleep.* With the final words—the plea for the Lord to take my soul *if I should die before I wake*, she touched my forehead and pulled the covers to my chin—*amen*—and slipped out the door, leaving it open a crack so the light from the kitchen shone in and the sounds of her clinking cutlery back into the drawer, dishes back into the cupboard told me where I was in the world. But in the upper bunk of the fifth-wheel trailer, with the firelight flaring and waning and sparks popping into the darkness, no mother crept down the stairs, no shadow floated out the door.

One of the men—Aldo or Bruno or Mr. Petrović—started to sing. His baritone voice, clear and bright, rang out in a language I didn't understand, and soon his fellow Croatians, who had come from so far away, leaving behind bloodshed and war, joined him in singing. Together their voices made a sound both sad and happy, full of hunger, soaked in wine, singing about the homeland they had left behind. When I pressed my face against the window screen, I saw my mother at the picnic table with the other wives, their backs to the flames and the men. In that circle around the fire, my dad hunched in a lawn chair, elbows on his knees, a cigarette hanging in one hand, a squat brown bottle in the other, his ballcap low to hide his eyes—and the song drawing us in, taking us all away— through the darkness and over the waters.

Rules of War

◇◇◇

IN THE MUSTY heat of the canvas tent, I sat brushing Malibu Barbie's shiny blonde hair, wishing for a gun. Outside, through the trees and in the yard, my brother and the neighbour boys tore around, their weapons slung over their backs as they dodged back and forth across enemy lines. Instead of fighting alongside them in their war game, I was listening to Carrie and Bonnie invent reasons for the Barbies to change their clothes. A doctor's appointment. A meeting at the bank. They flexed and twisted their dolls' arms and legs, snapping and unsnapping skinny pantsuits, pencil skirts, and flouncy gowns. A surprise birthday party. A horse ride on Dixie, the dream pony. A trip to the grocery store. They chattered happily, as if these storylines were the only ones worth following.

"GIRLS! GIRLS YOUR age!" my mother had declared when a family with two daughters moved into the empty house down our rural road. Within days of their arrival, she had introduced herself to the new neighbours and invited the girls for an afternoon of play. Up our driveway the pair came, each carrying what looked like a miniature suitcase.

"We brought our Barbies," they said. The brightness in their voices made me wary. Carrie, in a pink-and-white-striped T-shirt with matching pink shorts, was tall and thin, dark-haired. Her younger sister, Bonnie, wore the same short set in red. They seemed to have walked out of the pages of the Sears catalogue, clean and combed and glossy, smiling and without guile, the kind of girls who made me feel uneasy, awkward in my girl-ness.

I led them to our old cabin tent, which my mom had erected on a flat patch of grass beside the garden—"Like a playhouse!" she said. Once inside, we sat in a triangle, facing each other, waiting for something to happen.

I reached for the green mosquito coil smouldering in the corner. "Smell this." I held it up to them for a sniff.

Carrie and Bonnie pinched their noses and drew back. "Ew!" said Bonnie. "It stinks!"

"It's poison," I said, with triumph. "If you eat it, you'll die." Neither girl seemed impressed.

Carrie unclasped the metal buckles on her case and opened it to reveal a nest of dolls and dresses and tiny plastic accessories. "Let's play," she said, and handed me a Barbie in a turquoise swimsuit. "This one has her own sunglasses and everything," she said. "You can be her."

I WAS USED to being one girl in a pack of boys, following like a dog behind the hunters, crashing through the bush of our back acres, searching out the enemy. My brother and the other boys from our rural neighbourhood—Kenny and Gordy from through the trees, Marvin from Poplar Road, Santana and Ira, the scary Sinclair brothers—dictated the terrain and the kind of war we waged, whether on foot within the boundaries of the yard and its outbuildings—garden, pigpen, tree fort, garage—or off into the wild on kid-sized motorbikes.

We fought by a shared code, rules of war concocted after much consideration. No sissy time-outs. One gun per player, plus whatever grenades—pinecones and dried mud clots—you could carry. We built our guns by hand. A scrap of lumber tossed on the burn pile became the body of a gun, sanded smooth to stave off slivers. A length of old pipe or rebar got hacksawed into a barrel and scope. With the drill press in our dad's shop, my brother fit the barrel to the frame, polishing the metal until it shone. Finally, with a ballpoint pen, we inked the make and serial number into the wood, registering every weapon in our cache.

Each gun had its own noise, depending on the model. From the stuttered nasal *eh eh eh eh eh* of the semi-automatic, to the low, plosive front-teeth-tucked-inside-the-bottom-lip fire of the submachine gun, to the high-pitched volley and descent of the tossed explosive, our battlefield noises defined us. The ferocity and authenticity of the sound effect contributed to the soldier's credibility and threat. For the boys, the noises came naturally, as if they'd been born with mouths formed for the violence of this music. They shifted with ease between weapons, from Uzi to sniper rifle to .44 Magnum, their spit flying as they fired. No matter how much I practiced the *kackackackackackackackack* of my AK-47, my bullet stutter never was as loud and powerful as theirs, but it seemed enough to keep me in the war.

I'd be on my belly, army-crawling over the forest floor, wet dirt caked on the front of my shirt, camouflaged by the stinkweed and saplings, when ahead, from behind a stump, an enemy popped up, surveying for movement. If I stilled myself, ignoring the black flies that wheedled around my head, if I held my breath and made myself a stone, my enemy might move on, veer down some other trail blazed through the birch and poplar. But if I shifted the wrong way, snapped a twig, sniffed too loudly or swatted at the insect swarm, the gun found me. One way or another, whether by Marvin's fully-automatic *dakkadakkadakka* or by Gordy's *pew pew pew*, I was done, it was over. After the shooter yelled, "You're dead!" I lay on my back, eyes closed, clutching my imaginary gut wound as I bled out, and started counting to one hundred, the only way to bring myself to life again and back into the battle.

IT WAS KENNY'S idea to introduce hostage-taking to the game. "It'll be like real war," he said, "like in Russia or Yugoslavia."

"Or like how 007 gets captured and tied up," said Gordy, Kenny's little brother. He yanked up his T-shirt. "For your eyes only!" he said, and flashed his scrawny chest, then began to laugh so hard, he fell to the ground and pounded the dirt with his fists.

With a stick, Kenny dragged an X in the clay to mark our start, and then explained the new rule of engagement. In real war, soldiers didn't just automatically shoot the enemy dead. In real war, soldiers took people prisoner and held them at gunpoint until someone rescued them, or they got killed. "It'll be fun," he said.

After we picked our teams—Gordy and me, the youngest, left at the end to choose each other—we bolted from the X, scattering in all directions to race down trails and through the trees, leaping stumps, brush and thistle, singing in our heads—*one Mississippi, two Mississippi, three*—counting down toward the opening of war, I found a deadfall log to crouch behind. As I cooled my thumping heart and slowed my breathing, I scanned for enemies ahead, my assault rifle propped and ready to fire. The brush behind me crackled with someone's footsteps.

"Hands in the air," the voice said. The tip of a gun barrel knocked against my shoulder. "Stand up!"

When I turned around, Kenny was grinning, triumphant over me, the war's first prisoner. I was his, he said, his hostage, and I'd be the bait to bring in a rescuer so he could kill him, too. Kenny marched me toward the tree fort, headquarters, prodding me every few feet with his gun, telling me to keep quiet, or else.

In the bottom floor of the tree fort, as Kenny wound old rope around my hands and feet, I felt the strange thrill of the unknown, but a little fear, too, at how real it all felt—the rope scratching my wrists, a strip of cloth tied as a gag over my mouth. Kenny pulled down the rope ladder and clambered up to the top storey.

He looked down at me through the hole in the floor before letting the trap door shut. "Don't move," he said. "Or else."

Or else what, I didn't know, but his voice held the threat of a growl. Boys could do that with their voices, could make them go low and menacing so other boys perked up and girls backed down. Boys were stealthy as foxes, agile as rats. They climbed with an ease I longed to possess, up trees, ropes, ladders, forever up and up. They rode full-throttle to the crest of a hill they called Kamikaze, and left me in the gulley. In winter, they stood at the top of the snow pile and taunted, *You're no king of the castle—you're a girl.* No matter how many times I tried to reach the peak, one of them—Kenny, Marvin, Ira, my brother—sent me back down to the bottom.

Girls at the bottom, boys on top. Girls on this side, boys on the other. I had begun to notice the line drawn between us, to see that it was darkening, deepening into a trench. On the playground, at the bus stop, at Sunday-school choir practice, the girls clustered in their own giggling world while the boys huddled together, talking and laughing over jokes. I craned to hear from the outskirts, suspicious that I was missing out on something important, some secret that could crack the system's code. But the whole system seemed built on a broken foundation. Everywhere I looked, I saw the widening split. At our church-run school every Friday afternoon, all the students divided into groups for what the teachers called "Arts and Crafts." We girls funneled into age-appropriate activities like macramé, crocheting, embroidery, and other domestic arts. While the boys took part in outdoor survival, learning how to set a trap, build a snow shelter, and start a winter fire with only one wooden match, I sat in a semicircle of girls in a quiet room indoors, watching our volunteer craft leader, one of the church grandmas, demonstrate basic cross-stitch. How to thread the needle. How to read the pattern's design. How to sew a row of diagonal stitches, then double back and make them into a chain of X's. I bent over the gingham fabric held taut inside the embroidery hoop and drew the needle up and down, cross-stitching the tiny cells, X on X, like all the other girls.

More than the scent of Love's Baby Soft perfume, I loved the whiff of sulphur smoke wafting from the cap gun's barrel. More than the crochet hook, the pocketknife, and how it whittled a willow branch to a perfect spear. I played the games that most girls liked—house, office, beauty salon—but tired quickly of their scripts. Always, the house needed cleaning and the babies needed changing. The secretary answered the telephone for her boss. The hairdresser said, "I have just the style in mind!"

All the way back to Genesis and that first garden, my future seemed rigged. I tried to count my ribs to see if the story was true—that I'd been made the same as Eve, fashioned from a borrowed rib. Had the Creator's hand really reached down to Adam's sleeping body and unclipped one from its cage? I imagined God stewing that bone in the dust until it gathered steam, His breath like magic on it, and then in a whirl of mist, *poof*!—a woman. But I always lost track in my counting, and could never figure out how many ribs made up a girl.

I didn't want to be a boy; I only wanted entry to a boy's world. Full access. To do without restraint what boys could do. I wanted to shoot the moose, kindle the fire, rev the engine, and then come home to my pink-walled room, flop on my bed, and crack open my Trixie Belden mystery to see what clues the girl detective might sleuth out to solve the secret of the haunted mansion. I wanted to erase the line scuffed in the dust and go back to the beginning, before the world split in two. I wanted to pull from my body the borrowed rib and give it back, or better yet, for that borrowed rib to mark me as one of a band of brothers—and sisters, all of us built from the same breath and blood, bone of the same bone, flesh of the same flesh.

THE WAR WENT on without me in the field. Above me, Kenny fired his M-16—a vocal barrage of bullets—and launched explosives out the window with a shrill whistle and subsequent *kaboom!* When Gordy tried to get close enough to the tree fort to spring me loose, Kenny pulled an all-out assault. Through a knothole in the wall, he let loose a stream of urine, peeing on his little brother as he passed below, which triggered the other boys to raucous laughter, sent Gordy raging back at them with a stick-turned-machete, hacking at their backs, and left me in the dark.

Whatever thrill I'd felt at the start had fizzled. I was the only prisoner, which seemed boring and unfair. I was the only tagalong straggler, too, the lone girl added to the pack because *no one gets left out*, so said my mother, even when my brother huffed and rolled his eyes and argued for his freedom. For now, he had to take me with him into the wild world of boys, but in my hostage state, I felt it—that world tilting, shaking me loose from its adventure, and sending me to the other side of the dividing line.

Though the rope cinched around my wrists and ankles was thin and frayed, though I surely had enough muscle to break free of my makeshift chains, stand up, kick open the door on its flimsy hinges and bolt through the trees with my weapon ready, bolt for the hill and race to the top, to claim it, call it mine, my new ground, I didn't even try. No one had talked of escape as an option. I hunkered in the windowless dungeon of the tree fort and waited for rescue, or for someone's mom to call out, *Suppertime!*—and send us all back home.

INSIDE THE SUN-COOKED tent, with the screen door zipped to keep out bugs, we readied our dolls for an evening on the town. Bonnie stood her Barbie up and wiggled the doll back and forth. "I need a new hairdo," she said, her voice high and breathy. She dug through the pile of accessories and pulled up a tiny plastic mirror. She fitted it into the hand of her Barbie, who held it up to her face.

Carrie slid her doll's feet, forever fixed on tiptoes, into a pair of silver heels. "To match her silver dress," she said.

We girls played out our story, shadows of a sisterhood more ancient than we knew, of tents alive with other girls who sat inside and waited for a voice to call them out, for the broken world to reconcile, girls who sat inside and peered through the opening to see the moon and the path in darkness by which the men came home to them, carrying the meat and blazing torches.

I kept brushing my borrowed Barbie's plastic golden hair, listening for what came next.

Outside, from the trails cut through the forest at our backs, my brother and the boys yelled their war. Laughter from the bushes. Gunfire from the trees.

Taking Up the Remnants

◇◇◇

I CAN STILL SMELL the bridge's greasy wood cooked by summer sun, the scent of forest and fuel, and when the wind angled a particular way, the cool fishiness of the river beneath. As logging trucks rumbled over the structure, shaking the frame and winging sawdust and grit from their loads, the Nechako River flowed on, twisted and snaked, swirled with eddies that threated to pull a child under. *One death by drowning every summer*, said my mother, *don't let it be you.* The river that divided the town into north and south also stitched it together. The same current that cut the land in half bound us to its shores.

Until I was five, we lived off Loop Road, on the north side of the Nechako. Who built the house, how much my parents paid for it, the style of its construction—these facts meant nothing to me in those early years. Home was the way the curtains lifted with the open window's breeze. The crystal butter dish tucked behind the sugar. The blue glass hen on a nest filled with lemon drops. Home was my mother singing along to the vinyl LP spinning on the stereo, *Chanson d'amour, ra da da da*, and my brother and I taking turns holding the black dog's paws for a dance. Home was my dad awake at two AM for another night shift in the bush, him sitting at the dining room table, a cigarette balanced on the glass ashtray and a cup of coffee in one hand, and my mother standing at the kitchen counter in her turquoise housecoat, loading food into his huge black lunchbox.

Home was the kids who lived around us—Rachelle and Mallory, Wendy and Phoebe and their wild cousin Isaac— and the sandbox between our yards, the swing my dad hung between two poplar trees, and the rutted uphill driveway that led to Loop Road. Turn right to walk to Grandma Reimer, who lived with her two bachelor sons. Keep going to the Castellos and their skinny mutt that strained at the end of a chain and snarled at anyone who passed. Farther still, where Loop Road met Northside, lived Tante Nite—my father's eldest sister—and her family. Down left of us, my mother's sister lived with her family, grain-farming the river-frontage acres. Down farther, more cousins, more aunts, uncles, folks from church, and next door, the game warden and his wife, and their baby.

When we rode our bicycles together along the shoulder of Loop Road, the game warden's wife always took the lead. She strapped her infant daughter into a plastic seat on the back of her bike, and over her handlebars, carried a long stick with a nail hammered through one end. To any dog that chased and snapped at our ankles, she gave one swoop of the stick, the nail-end whooshing down through air to strike the dog's rump. A yelp, a blur of fur flying away from us down the gravel road—and the animal tore back to its doghouse and old soup bone.

Around and around the loop, we walked, ran, pedaled, and drove. Every house had a name, a story, a barking dog. At Uncle George's trailer two driveways over, my mother caught the oldest Castello boy jumping out the window, a jar of coins in his clutch, and hauled him back to our kitchen, threatening to call the cops if he tried to flee. *Shame on you*, she said, and telephoned Uncle George to come, then offered the boy something to eat while he waited for his reprimand.

On Loop Road, I learned to ride the orange banana-seat bike without training wheels, learned to pump my legs to make the swing arc higher through its pathway in the trees. On Loop Road, I slipped pieces of Juicy Fruit gum to Phoebe through the wire fence after she fell out of their moving car, her shins dragging along the gravel as she clung to the passenger door, and came back from the hospital bandaged and unable to walk for weeks. *And that's why you need to keep your seat belt buckled*, said my mother, pointing out through my bedroom window at Phoebe, who lay on a blanket in her backyard trying not to cry, her raw, oozing legs smeared white with ointment. *Good thing she didn't lose them*, my mother said, and I pictured a legless Phoebe pulling herself across the lawn for another stick of gum.

Memory drags back its bits of bone, handfuls of dust, surfaces like snapshots in a crawlspace scrapbook buried by years, a broken line of a song whose melody keeps playing, the image of a dream upon waking. Pluck one memory from the album and the story doesn't hold, won't bear up. The single part won't speak the whole. But honour the fragments, all those broken pieces, and see them find a true design, fitting to the pattern of a bigger story, no matter how small the town, the life, or the child.

To go back to the ground of my making, to stand inside that world again and sift those early years, see what's left, what stories lift, who speaks, who sings, what haunts and shimmers into sight—this salvaging illuminates the days ahead, and pieces together—*re-members*—the shape of what's to come. In a future house, away from Loop Road and south over the river, the train tracks, and up the hill, I'd stand again, holding on to every little scrap and wonder, every stitch and scar, listening to my mother sing the same song in a different kitchen, my brother holler from a new acre of poplars and pine, to the black dog barking and my dad's truck rumbling up the drive, air brakes hissing as he pulled into the yard, kicking up the dust.

In my earliest memory, I wake to the scrape of my belly over the wooden side of the crib and the *whump* of me landing on blue carpet. *Shh*, my brother says, his dark eyes before me, finger to his lips. He takes my hand, and down the dim hallway, I follow. The back door swings open to daylight and the green world. He leaps from the doorway—disappears, and leaves me standing on the threshold, teetering mid-air at the drop-off, the staircase not yet built. *Jump*, his voice says, and his hands stretch up to me. I crouch, fall forward, slide into his arms, through his grip, down his body, and land, wobbling, on ground, barefoot, grass-prickle between my toes, sunshine in my eyes.

The photograph my mother took shows me in a white dress smocked with red stitching. My white-blonde hair sticks up from my sweaty head in tufts. I squint beside my brother, three years older than me and brown-haired, brown-eyed, olive-skinned, both of us caught in the act of escaping from our afternoon nap. In the next photo, I'm smiling with a wide-open mouth, free to roam the yard with the black dog at my side, my brother, the punished, sent back to his room.

When called, memory comes back, but never whole. In pieces, it comes—this trinket, that strange perfume, this camera flash, that shred and remnant. *You can use anything from the rag bag*, said my mother, and held out for me the huge clear plastic bag overflowing fabric scraps, bits of lace, rickrack, and ribbon. At the kitchen table, I dumped it out. The world spilled out in pieces. A gingham strip from my embroidered pillowcase. A slip of vivid green Fortrel—my mother's dress, the birthday one with emerald buttons running down the bodice, the one she wears in the photograph of her and my father standing in front of his new logging truck, my brother still a baby, balanced on the bumper. The red and orange cotton of my nightgown's Raggedy Ann. My brother's navy corduroy from his pair of school pants.

I chose two calicos—mint green with rosebud sprigs, and red apples on a sky-blue check. With my mother's silver scissors, I cut them into matching squares, a little crooked on the edge, but close enough. I lay them side by side so that the colours sharpened, brightened, blue on green on pink on red, then flipped them front to front and pinned a seam. I slid the cloth underneath the needle's foot, locked it in position, ready to stitch.

Each evening after supper, my mother in the basement sewing room bent over her machine, mending what needed mending, altering what needed to fit. Around her neck, the measuring tape hung, and in her mouth, the heads of pins jutted out so that her lips glinted silver when the overhead light caught. Everything that ripped apart, she fixed, and from the old and worn-out, sewed something new. My dad's grease-stained jeans with the knees frayed thin became a denim camping blanket. Even my bedspread, pieced together from clothing I outgrew or the fabric scraps left over from their sewing, testified that anything could be salvaged and made new. Before she turned out the bedside lamp, my mother would point out the different patterns. This is from the dress you wore three Easters ago, she'd say, the one with the velvet bodice. This is the dress you called "Applejack." This was the jumpsuit you wore to Hawaii. This is the one from your first-grade Christmas concert.

At my own machine, the little chainstitch Singer for beginner sewers, I pressed the plastic pedal with my foot, and as the needle punched down and up, binding with its thread, I guided the fabric through and watched the pieces join, and when they did, I pulled more scraps from the overflowing bag—grey flowers on a stiff black cotton, gold stars on deep blue sky, sheer white as gauzy as a veil, still bearing hints of red smocking thread—remnants from a wider life, a bigger story, a patchwork quilt I'd sleep beneath, autumn, winter, spring, and summer, dreaming toward morning and the voice at the bedroom door calling me to wake up, sun's out, the food is on the table.

Acknowledgments

◇◇◇

I AM GRATEFUL FOR grants from the BC Arts Council and the Canada Council for the Arts, which allowed me time and space to write.

Earlier versions of "Rules of War," "The Lady of the Lake," "The Pledge," and "All the Ways to Fall" were published in *The Tyee* in September 2017.

Thank you to Jackie Kaiser and the team at Westwood Creative Artists for championing this project and welcoming me to their vibrant literary crew. To Greystone Books—thank you for enthusiastically embracing this book. Paula Ayer, your deft insights, keen editorial eye, and bright faith in my writing have been a gift.

And thank you to my stellar community of friends who cheered me on in the writing, who walked beside me and listened to me mull, and who corroborated and reminisced.

To Jeanine, and to Jo and Dave—thank you for your kindness and clarity of sight. A special thanks to Brother Rob, who daily stoked the fires behind the scenes, to Amelia, to Richard, to my mother, to Grandma Shenk, and to the whole family— those nearest on the tree and those on farther branches, for giving me the rich inheritance of story.

Most of all, thank you to Lance, my long-haul love, for making this marriage large and spacious, and for saying, *Write*.